Also by Dr. Nick Argyle:

From Anxiety to Peace, Choosing a Therapy for Anxiety and Panic: Behavioral, Cognitive, Group, Drugs, Natural Medicine, and Meditation.

"This enjoyable book elegantly summarizes different strategies for managing anxiety, explaining in clear and practical terms how they work and for whom they are most helpful. The tone is positive and hopeful, emphasizing that anxiety is eminently treatable, with many useful examples and practical insights drawn from the author's long experience at the frontline of clinical psychiatry.

A common theme is that difficulties are often best solved by bringing a second element to bear on the problem – darkness is dispelled by bringing light, not by investigating darkness.

From Anxiety to Peace shows how different therapies help the individual to move beyond the busy, fragmented, surface level of thinking – where worry and agitation are all too common – to utilize more fundamentals levels of mind and intellect, where thinking is naturally calmer, more integrated, harmonious, effective, and progressive.

As we learn new skills, we are utilizing more of the brain's vast potential. When the body is free from fatigue and imbalances, then the operational capacity of our brain is enhanced, leading to more rewarding experience, clearer thinking, and greater happiness."

Dr Roger Chalmers

From Depression to Bliss

The many therapies for depression

Establishing bliss in the mind

By

Dr. Nick Argyle

Copyright © 2017 by Nick Argyle

All Rights Reserved

A title from Grayle Books

Dedicated to Jacqueline who has given me so much happiness in my life

Acknowledgements

I thank all the great teachers in my clinical career for their wisdom. My patients have also taught me by sharing their own narratives. All references to individual patients or clients have been disguised to protect their privacy.

My knowledge of Vedic science comes from Maharishi Mahesh Yogi who has revived this ancient knowledge. I have gained knowledge from his teaching and experience through the Vedic techniques of consciousness including Transcendental Meditation.

I recognise that not every-one is comfortable with being called a "patient" preferring to be called a client, consumer or service user. "Patient" has a flavour of passivity and helplessness to some. I do use this term for the sake of familiarity but also to remember that the word has the original meaning of one who suffers.

Similarly I use "Doctor" for the therapist role but this should be taken to include medical doctors, psychologists and practitioners from the different schools covered in the book.

Table of Contents

Chapter 1
Depression – a Modern Pandemic Page 1

Chapter 2
All Work and No Play - The Behavioral Approach Page 21

Chapter 3
Seeing the Glass Half Full - Cognitive therapy Page 33

Chapter 4
Separation and Loss - Psychoanalytic Therapies Page 45

Chapter 5
Strength in Numbers - Group Therapy Page 67

Chapter 6
Magic Bullets - Biological Psychiatry Page 83

Chapter 7
Harmony with Nature - Natural Medicine Page 105

Chapter 8
The Science of Life - Maharishi Ayur Veda Page 129

Chapter 9
Discovering Inner Bliss - Transcendental Meditation Page 147

Chapter 10
Pathways from Depression to Bliss Page 167

Appendices and Further Reading Page 179

∞ Chapter 1 ∞
Depression – a Modern Pandemic

A great wave of enthusiasm is sweeping through modern psychiatry which is very fortunate because there is much work to do. Depression has become the disease of our time. It is already the third largest cause of disability in the world and is set to be number one by the year 2030. Mood disorder has become more common over the last century and now one person in five is likely to suffer a significant episode of depression in their life. This has prompted the World Health Organisation to remember that good health must include good mental health. The quality of our mental life is of central importance. Our mood can be better and it should be better. The good news is that there are many ways to treat depression so our challenge is to choose the right therapy.

Scientists have been looking for an "Agent Blue" to explain this increase in depression. Is this stress or could there be an infectious organism, or some toxic chemical in the environment? A more modern theory is of social contagion through our relationships and social networks. Perhaps the Internet is spreading more than just computer viruses.

Depression can be analysed from many perspectives. There are social and psychological factors. Your dog has died. Your teenage daughter has run away. Loneliness and a lack of engagement in society are also crucial. You excessively blame yourself for set-backs. There are political and economic factors with unemployment and poverty the most obvious. The biological approach is now very strong with anti-depressant drugs extremely fashionable but should we see depression as just a physiological illness to be cured? Is it a more of a social and political problem or should we perhaps look to our life-styles to improve our harmony with nature?

It is important to understand how different approaches to causation and cure can be integrated. This book examines the various paradigms and looks to their deeper principles. This enables us to see which therapies suit which people and types of depression.

We also take a lesson from another common problem, cardiovascular disease. Study of heart disease and strokes shows there are clearly several different factors: genetic predisposition, smoking, high blood pressure, cholesterol and lipids, glucose metabolism, obesity, and stress. Successful reduction of risk comes from looking at all the factors that are relevant for an individual or a whole population.

Because depression is experienced so subjectively we tend to look for psychological answers. These can be very relevant, but there may be other factors predisposing you to becoming depressed when that dog dies or that job is lost. To treat depression and prevent its recurrence we should look to several different areas just as we do in heart disease.

We can also look to the field of infectious health where there has been tremendous success with immunisation programmes and public sanitation to prevent illnesses. Mental health has found the question of prevention more difficult to answer. We know our society is mentally unclean with much stress, addiction, crime and conflict, but how to improve mental sanitation has been elusive. Education is one obvious place to increase resilience to stress and reduce the risk of addiction. Legislation, for example against drugs, has been notably unsuccessful. Can we improve mental hygiene and develop stronger more mature and fulfilled people who are resistant to depression? We can, but we need to go to a deeper level of the mind to achieve this.

Defining Depression

The core of depression is a low mood. We feel unhappy, sad, and tearful. An episode of depression is marked by a reduction from our normal mood. However what I accept as a normal mood for me may not be so normal. In other aspects of health such as blood pressure, weight, or cholesterol we know that the statistically normal or average for a population may be far from ideal or healthy. The same is true for mood. Sadly we have come to accept a low mood as being almost expected. Other companions of depression such as boredom, loneliness, low self-esteem and lack of meaning in life are also widespread. Therefore one type of depression is having a low baseline mood. This may escape notice because you see it as usual for you. Psychiatrists call this dysthymia or dysthymic personality. Luckily we no longer see personality as unchanging, but strategies targeting your long-term constitution and life-style will be rather different to treatments used for episodic depression.

Depression occurring in episodes is the more obvious form with your base-line mood between episodes being normal. These depressions last for several months but can become longer lasting. If you also have periods of abnormally high mood this is called Bipolar illness or Manic Depression. There are other periodic depressions linked to the natural rhythms of the menstrual cycle, the seasons, and child-birth.

Mood can also change over very short periods of time within a day or a few minutes. To some extent this is normal as we meet the ups and downs of daily life but excessive mood fluctuation is a common personality trait sometimes linked to a Borderline personality style. Adverse events lead to exaggerated mood swings which take longer to settle and are hard to self-soothe.

Depression is also categorised by whether or not it is precipitated by life events. "Reactive" depression comes after a loss or negative news whereas "Endogenous" episodes seem to arrive out of a clear sky and suggest a more genetic or internal causation. However the distinction is not always clear cut because if you have a genetic predisposition, life events can still be triggers for episodes to start.

There are additional physiological precipitating factors such as physical illness, alcohol and drugs, or natural hormonal swings. Often more than one factor is active in tipping us into a depression.

Another way to describe different forms of depression is in terms of symptom clusters. What do we experience other than our mood being low? Melancholia is characterised by low energy and concentration, lack of pleasure, loss of sleep and appetite. Non-melancholic depression, which is more common, shows more anxiety and distress with reduced work and social function but not so many physical symptoms as Melancholia. Melancholia is usually more severe, occurs equally in men and women, and requires more professional therapy. Non-melancholic depression is 50% commoner in women. A third symptom cluster is "Atypical" depression which has more relationship to life events and longer-standing personality vulnerabilities such as rejection sensitivity. It is called Atypical as eating and sleeping are increased.

Psychotic symptoms like hallucinations or delusions may occur and would suggest a more extreme illness often related to a Bipolar or Melancholic depression, drug-induced illness, or physical illness pushing our brain chemistry far out of balance.

This confusing variety of ways in which depressions can be divided up reflects the multiple possible factors behind any one person's depression.

Many causes of the blues

Depression runs in families and while there are several possible mechanisms behind this, research clearly shows a big genetic contribution. This is estimated to be around 40%, with the other 60% being environmental. This genetic evidence is stronger for Melancholia and Bipolar illness.

We do not yet have genetic therapy to repair risky genes but we increasingly see the effects of other factors on whether or not genes are expressed. If you have a strong family history of depression then clearly you are at increased risk. If you have already had depressive episodes, especially if other factors are not obvious, then you are at high risk of further depression. You need to look at all the other factors you can improve and which elements in your life-style can protect you from depression.

There are many external stresses which predispose to depression. The loss of a parent in childhood is one of the most tragic events with which to cope. Poverty is a major risk world-wide. Relationship stresses include having no close friend or relative to confide in or having an abusive alcoholic partner. Chronic illness, either mental or physical, makes depression more likely and harder to treat. Alcohol and illegal drugs are major and much ignored factors.

Some people seem to be just happier or more stable than others as part of their constitution. Personality traits which increase risk are being anxious, self-critical or sensitive to rejection. Tending to compare yourself unfavourably with others can be part of self-criticism but can also be a matter of where you put your attention. If you are always contemplating your neighbour's slightly newer BMW you do not feel great. It you think of the millions in the world who have to walk to get clean water every day you might feel differently about your situation. Counting your blessings used to be a healthy habit taught to children.

A less well recognised risk factor is being too focussed on external or material reward at the expense of inner or spiritual development. The modern world pushes external and active excitement as the way to enjoy life. Having the latest gadgets, a thousand friends on Facebook and going to endless parties only provides part of what we need to be happy. We also need to mature emotionally and spiritually.

From the perspective of evolution, anything which is common and persists through generations can be considered as having had some value to the individual or the tribe. In Bipolar disorder having a full-blown illness does not seem very useful as your functioning in daily life deteriorates and your perspective is unbalanced. Some artists do find inspiration and creativity in the extremes of mood but more commonly creative or useful work suffers. However there are often very successful people in the families of people with Bipolar illness, so a milder dose of Bipolar genes may be useful. Some of these people are hyper-thymic, that is their mood is higher than average; they need less sleep; their self-confidence is high. Optimism and risk-taking are traits which are useful at the right level. A group of people with some Bipolar traits have long periods of usefully high energy and confidence between periods of depression. Winston Churchill was a well-known example.

For depression which is neither Bipolar nor Melancholia women are more affected than men. This increased risk for women is most marked during the reproductive years. Again there are many suggested mechanisms ranging from the social roles of women to hormonal effects on the brain and bio-rhythms.

An evolutionary theory tries to account for the increased depression among women. Women contribute more to social cohesion among a tribal group but do so at the expense of their own mood. They compromise and look after others while putting their own needs aside. There is also evidence that where men have to acquiesce because they are lower down the male hierarchy they are more prone to depression.

The Diversity of Life

How can we best comprehend all the factors that may influence depression? There are many possible causes and even more types of therapy to choose from. The main areas of life can be summarised into the mind, body and environment. The environment includes both the physical surroundings and society which is comprised of other people and their minds.

We live in a world of differences both outside in our geography and society and inside in our thoughts and feelings. Consciousness is the underlying field of intelligence which rests beneath the diversity of mental life. Intelligence seems divided between the subjective and objective spheres. We experience the subjective side of intelligence directly in our own minds. We intellectually understand objective intelligence in the laws of nature, manifest in the outside world. The main areas of life are shown on the chart along with the main principles of therapy: balance, synchrony, connectedness and transcending.

On the objective side, many scientists have become interested in consciousness because the universe no longer seems to them to be just a complicated machine. The intelligence, dynamism, and creativity inherent in the laws of nature are much more suggestive of consciousness. Throughout the ages artists and people from spiritual traditions have experienced and expressed this transcendental level of life.

Unified Field Chart for Mental Health

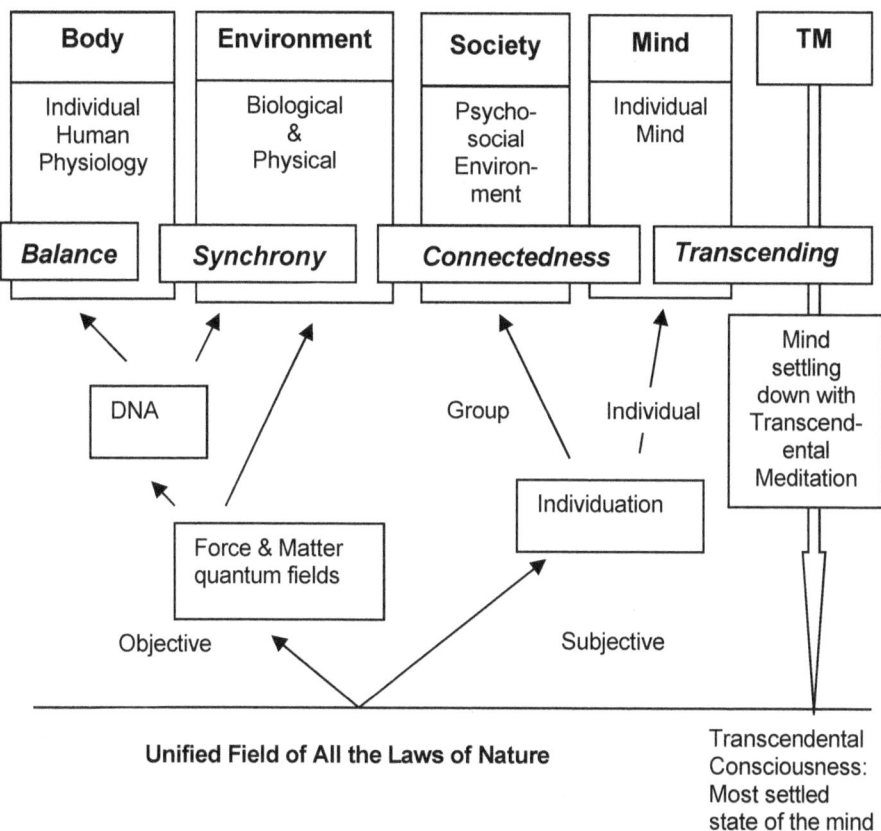

In the Vedic tradition there are simple mental techniques like Transcendental Meditation to facilitate the individual's mind experiencing its own inner nature. This corresponds on the chart to the mind settling down to its most settled state which is the underlying field of consciousness itself.

The Body

The biological and physical sciences form a strong scientific paradigm because they are well integrated. The different layers of the body's organs, tissues, cells, and molecules are all well connected in our scientific model. Causes for depression are seen especially at the level of individual chemicals, hormones and neuro-transmitters with the main therapeutic aim being to achieve a normal balance of chemicals. Unfortunately the complexity of the myriad chemicals and cells in the body means that our knowledge of this level is incomplete so drugs do not always work or may have side-effects.

Main Areas of PHYSICAL Therapy
Exercise
Balancing the constitution
Stablizing biological rhythms
Treating physical illness
Balancing hormones
Balancing neuro-transmitters

At a more superficial level we need to balance the amount of activity and rest – a simple idea which has been forgotten in our sophisticated busy modern world.

Natural Medicine also emphasises balance and may use different languages of energy channels or constitutional tendencies. These do not translate easily into a chemical language but constitutional typing from natural systems can be a more practical summary of our tendencies than a chemical genetic analysis currently gives us.

Genetics is seen as our deepest level of modern scientific enquiry in the physiology and in terms of chemical intelligence there is no deeper. But there are other fields of intelligence that are more profound. We now need to connect biology to the deeper levels of modern physics. In a scientific sense, chemistry is the basis of biology, the basis of chemistry is physics, and the fundamental basis of physics is Quantum Theory. The deeper theories of physics such as Quantum Theory and Unified Field Theory describe levels of intelligence beyond the observable objective world. At the basis of our physical world is a field of intelligence that interacts with itself and has spontaneous creativity. Modern physicists are happy to discuss the parallel between this intelligence, the finest level of the objective world, and that intelligence which we experience in our minds subjectively.

The Mind

The psychological sciences have been much less integrated than the biological sciences. This is due partly to a failure of understanding and partly to political conflict. Everyone is convinced their school of thought is the best with some therapies being so dogmatic that they have been called "psycho-theologies".

> **MENTAL Therapies**
> Balance of rewarding activities
> Better cognitive styles
> Achieving goals
> Problem solving
> Positive relationships
> Dealing with loss
> Finding meaning
> Self-realization

Even the basic structure of the mind is unclear. There is no equivalent to the simple structure of chemicals making up cells making up organs and the whole body. Are depressive thoughts or sad feelings more fundamental? Should therapy focus on patterns of thinking or emotions or relationships?

Behavior is the most superficial aspect of mind. Behavior Therapy is a mainstay of anxiety therapy but is less used in depression. It may be used informally as we try to get more rest or find more rewarding activities. Cognitive Therapy changes our thinking patterns and requires us to think about our own thoughts, a special human ability. Analytic therapies emphasise emotions and relationships and propose that unconscious parts of the mind need to be made available for self-knowledge. At a deeper level there are therapies which look into the development of the spiritual level and the transcendental aspect of the mind which goes beyond our individuality.

Summarising the principles of the psychological therapies is not so easy. Balance is still important, between types of activity, ways of thinking and between thinking and feeling. Regarding the individual's relationships with others, separation and loss are main drivers of depression so connectedness is a strong antidote. In psychological therapies the fundamental strategy is stepping back to look at your behaviour, thoughts, feelings or relationships. Moving our perspective to a deeper level is called transcending. Most therapies encourage stepping back enough to better observe our surface thoughts or feelings and some delve further into the unconscious mind. With a more profound technique like TM the emphasis is on experiencing the most settled area of the mind and experiencing the field of consciousness itself.

Society

Social isolation and loss of role are definite factors in depression. We are social beings and need to connect to others and contribute to our community. The absence of loving supportive relationships predisposes us to depression and if this occurs in childhood the risk of future depression is much higher. Abuse often leads to depression and this is more than the absence of support as often the abuser is also in a position of power or a supposedly caring role, whether at work or home, and is not easily escaped.

> **SOCIAL Therapies**
> Role satisfaction in work and family
> Connecting to others
> Supportive culture
> Freedom from abuse
> Society having higher goals

Poverty brings the additional stress of lacking the basic necessities of food and housing. World-wide this is a major factor in depression but curiously the increase in the depression has been well recorded in societies that are becoming wealthier. This speaks of a lack of connectedness and direction for society as a whole. Whether or not money can buy you love, it does not seem to buy much happiness once you are above the poverty line. We need to find higher goals once our basic needs are met.

Environment

As with the physical body, the environment is complex and we find several candidates here for Agent Blue. Are chemical pollutants to blame? Can a return to organic agriculture save us? Are viruses causing depression? Many societies are awash with alcohol and illegal drugs which are known to

> **ENVIRONMENTAL Therapies**
> Clean air, water and food
> Resistance to infection
> Avoiding alcohol and drug damage
> Balanced diet
> Synchrony with natural rhythms
> Healthy architecture

affect mood. Our reluctance to address addiction is a tribute to the power of our collective denial.

One pervasive aspect of the environment is time and the rhythms of life. We have poor synchrony with the natural rhythms of day and night or the seasons and there is good evidence that being out of rhythm is a promoter of depression. The pattern of space around us in our buildings and urban planning may be as important as the rhythms of time and life-supporting architecture is a growing field of interest.

Diet is another area where the vast number of different molecules makes chemical analysis very complex which is partly why modern science has only recently become interested in the role of food to alter mood. Advice on food is a major approach in natural systems of medicine and plant-based remedies remain prominent in many countries.

The Unified Field of Intelligence

The structure of the Unified Field can be said to be the laws of nature. All the intelligence that runs the physical universe is contained within the quantum fields and within the Unified Field. This is the basic level of intelligence where all the different laws or strands of intelligence are completely integrated. Vedic Science is clear that conscious phenomena or experiences are also based in the unified field of consciousness and this field is identical to the Unified Field of physics underlying objective reality. Many physicists have taken their studies beyond the material world to that of pure intelligence and have seen the parallels between the Unified Field and consciousness.

Doctors and medical scientists are still caught up in the detail of life, in the classical world. Even in psychiatry, where the mind-body link should be central, the fundamental relationship between the subjective and objective worlds is seen as too difficult to understand.

Experiencing the transcendent

To experience this deeper state of consciousness we take to meditation. There are many forms of meditation relating to different levels of the mind. Transcendental Meditation (TM) is a simple technique to allow the mind's attention to go to deeper and deeper levels, diving to the most settled transcendental level. All individual thoughts are transcended. This parallels the progress of science through time to find knowledge at deeper and deeper levels. Science has now travelled beyond time and space and beyond individual particles to transcendental fields of intelligence and natural law. Our direct experience can also transcend beyond individual thought to Pure Consciousness, transcending time and space and any relative content of consciousness. This is the experience of the field of consciousness itself.

The nature of consciousness

We shall look at the deeper principles of different schools of therapy in later chapters but what can be said of the fundamental character of consciousness itself? Consciousness has as its defining characteristic the ability to know itself. When we wake up in the morning, we are not passive computers, waiting for input. Even if we have no specific thought or sensation we are awake and aware of being ourselves.

This self-interacting dynamic gives rise to the diversity of its expressions. When we have a thought consciousness appears to split into the Knower, the process of Knowing, and the Known. This results in the division of subjective and objective fields of life. Similarly, the mind, the body, and the environment seem very separate. Individual people appear completely distinct. It is the interplay within consciousness between the Knower, the process of Knowing, and the Known that gives rise to these differences.

The Knower, process of Knowing, and the Known

When I think a thought, there appear to be three different elements. Firstly there is 'I' who is the thinker or observer; secondly, the thinking or observing process; and thirdly, the thought or the object of observation. The thinker and the thought are both within consciousness, as is the process of thinking. Similarly, when we have sensory experience, there is an observer, process of observation, and object. While there may be an object out there, the perception is experienced within our consciousness.

All three aspects are fluctuations in the same field. They appear separate. The unity of consciousness appears to have been lost. It is more understandable that external objects and other people seem separate but this seems to be the case even for our own thoughts. When depressive thoughts and feelings are so separate from our self then they have the power to over-shadow and distress us so we feel helpless even to control the content of our own minds. This apparent separation is called the mistake of the intellect in the Vedic Tradition. It has no name in modern psychology as recent traditions deal with differences of thought, emotions and action and not with the unity of the mind.

Unity does not have to be lost. When the mind retains the feeling of unity at the same time as discriminating differences this is a positive blissful experience. Experiencing another person as being so close they are not separate is an experience of love. The other person is as close and dear as one's self.

Knower, Knowing and Known therapies

The main areas of therapy can be divided according to which aspect of consciousness they focus on. The table gives an overview.

Therapies which improve the Knower side of our mind increase our consistency and strength of experience for our observing self. Stepping back to look at our own thoughts is the first element of Cognitive Therapy. It is also possible to know other peoples' thoughts and ideas through Psycho-education. This could be from a book, the internet or a class. Many individual therapies also have some didactic component.

When the small individual self is healthier we enjoy more self-efficacy to improve our own mood and lessen helplessness. The larger Self is found through having a perspective that goes well beyond the changing levels of individual thoughts and negative emotions. This side to life has been lost in some cultures where individual wealth and material possessions are worshipped.

Mindfulness may start us in this direction. Transcendental Meditation is a more reliable path to the deepest level of the mind.

	Aspects of Consciousness		
	Knower	**Knowing**	**Known**
Individual level of life	Cognitive Therapy	Psychoanalysis and process psychotherapies	Biological Psychiatry
Group level of life	Psycho-education (not always in a group but best suited to groups or available to many over internet)	Family and Group Therapy	Behavior Therapy (most important behaviors do involve other people)

Enhancing the Process of Knowing is found in Psychoanalysis and related psychotherapies which are called "process" therapies. Individual therapies deal to the internal dynamics of one person's mind. Our ability to process emotions and relationships improves and thinking is less distorted by conflicts or abnormal mood. We can set better goals and are better equipped to reach them.

Groups and families also have dynamics between individuals and family therapies work with these relationships. The therapist enters into the family system to help its members see things differently or from a new perspective stimulating change in behavior and interactions.

The more superficial Known aspects of our life are the physical body and our behavior both of which are expressions of our inner intelligence. Balancing our internal chemistry or our activity are both ways to strengthen the Known aspects of life. These are the more material and objective aspects of our life. As such they are easier to measure with modern science and the research evidence for Biological Psychiatry especially is strong in terms of the scientific method.

Knowledge and experience

Within any particular therapy a patient will take up different positions through time. Typically we start with some orientation and education about the therapy's theory and approach. This requires the patient to be in the Knower role listening to the Doctor. Then the patient is involved in detailing their symptoms which requires them to enter more of the Knowing role helping analyse their situation. A diagnosis is arrived at which becomes a Known aspect of the patient and this should also include their strengths and environment. The next phase is active therapy which may be a pill, practicing a behavior or new types of thinking, experiencing the relationship with the therapist, or life-style change. All of these are direct experiences which are in the Known area of life. Next there is some feedback and review which has the patient back in the Knowing role discussing progress with the therapist. Then there is consolidation to ensure knowledge is understood and owned by the patient who is now back in the Knower role. The hope is that this cycle leads to an integration of knowledge into the wholeness of the patient's improved mental life.

This cycle takes the patient from knowledge to experience and back. Both are needed for progress and the cycle may be repeated many times. If we look at therapies which we put in the Known area, Biological Psychiatry and Behavior Therapy, these would typically start with some education and analysis, with the patient in the Knower and Knowing roles, but they do not have to. Behavior therapy can be applied to people who are unaware it is happening such as children and people with dementia. Similarly drug therapy can be applied without discussion though of course this would be unusual. In the Knowing area therapies a practitioner very dedicated to the importance of process might also skip any introduction, remaining silent and allowing the patient or family to choose where they started.

Doctor – Patient Relationships

The interaction of Knower, Knowing and Known sounds abstract and benefits from more illustration. One theme running through the book is this doctor-patient relationship. The relationships and interactions between a doctor and patient are played out by their assuming different roles. Different patterns arise from the ways that doctors and patients learn from each other. Your doctor may examine you as an object, be an example to be observed by you, or represent the process through which you look at yourself.

This relationship between the doctor and patient is recognized as important in all types of therapy and seen as absolutely central in many psychological theories. Medical doctors are permitted to interact with patients' bodies in ways that are not expected in other relationships. In the same way psychiatrists and psychologists are allowed and taught to interact with patients' minds in special ways. The different basic interactions between Doctor and Patient can be seen to give rise to the different schools or approaches in modern psychiatry.

In a traditional medical model the Doctor observes and examines the Patient. He has the expert knowledge and does not share this with the passive Patient. Clearly the Doctor is the Knower and the Patient the Known. In psychological therapies we generally try to push the Patient towards the Knower position. This is partly to overcome passivity and helplessness but also to allow them to gain knowledge for which they will retain ownership. Psychoanalysis is the classic example of this where the Doctor, or Analyst, answers your question with another question, encouraging a process of Knowing leading to self-knowledge and the establishment of the patient as Knower of themselves. In Behavior Therapy the therapist acts as a model, the Known, for the patient to observe and primarily wants the patient to copy, to act, and to learn, experience being more important than intellectual knowledge.

Integrating Knower, Knowing and Known

For a patient to become fully well they need to achieve a balance of Knower, Knowing and Known in themselves. If the biological doctor retains the entire Knower role, or the Psychotherapist retains all of the process role, then the patient remains dependent and cannot become whole. Therapy should aim to enliven all three aspects in the patient. In psychoanalysis the experience of new self-knowledge is seen as special and named "insight". Analysis recognizes that self-knowledge is only truly useful when validated and owned by the patient. Overcoming conflicts and division in the mind, caused ultimately by the mistake of the intellect, is not solely an intellectual process but requires direct experience of increased integration.

Even in the medical model there is a higher expectation today that knowledge will be shared with the Patient and access to information over the Internet has accelerated this trend.

Aiming higher

The study of evolution in psychiatry has been concerned with the past. It has considered how psychological skills honed in the jungle fit into an urban society today. We should also be asking how far evolution has now taken us. There is plenty of evidence that we are not making use of the potential we already have in our brains. From the perspective of evolution human brains are surprisingly big, especially the forebrain. Some neuro-scientists have been puzzled as to what it is all there for. Currently it does not look so much as if mental problems are due to a lack of evolution and the need for a newer model. Rather it seems that we are missing the handbook for the model that we have. We are only living in a few rooms seemingly unaware of the rest of the great mansion that we already inhabit. One the one hand the recently evolved areas of the brain seem under stress, on the other hand we do not seem to be fully using them. This indicates that the brain has made a leap in evolution but we are still discovering our new mental potential.

One important higher function is the ability to step back or transcend and reflect on our own thoughts and feelings. This allows us to monitor, plan, and change – all important for mental success. An extension of this ability is our capacity to step even further back and to transcend to the mind's most settled state of simple awareness or Pure Consciousness. We shall see in a later chapter the health benefits from experiencing this level of the mind.

We live in mentally vulnerable times. Previous supports from the village, the church and family have weakened. The nation state is weaker so our identity here is also less secure. The twentieth century saw the rise of the individual, the single personality. This has allowed some amazing achievements but at a cost. If the individual is all, then who is to blame when things go wrong? It is you yourself and when failure is all blamed on the self then depression results. Depression indeed has been the epidemic of the last century. In response we have had Prozac and Cognitive Therapy to try to replace helplessness with 'Learned Optimism' but more is needed.

The idea that depression is normal must be challenged. It is one thing to have transient negative emotions or reactions but another for these to overwhelm us and cause distress or disability. We should be looking to self-development and education through which we can become resilient enough and mature enough to truly enjoy life. This means not just intellectual development but also emotional maturity and spiritual fulfilment.

A higher standard of mental health is needed which encompasses much more than the reduction of depressive symptoms. Modern psychiatry is already traveling down this path. As we turn our attention to the general population it becomes even more obvious that higher goals are necessary. The average or normal mood of the population needs raising. Such improved mental health requires full maturity to overcome the conflicts and differences apparent in life. There is already strong evidence that techniques are available to promote such maturity and enlightenment.

Summary

In this book we look at all the main approaches to treating depression. This allows you to understand which factors are influencing your mood and there are likely to be more than one. You need to recognise that even when there is one obvious cause it is worth looking at other contributing factors. Knowledge of the various factors guides you to changes in your thinking, behaviour or life-style which can counteract depression. It is important to choose wisely, especially as many therapists are experts only in their own tradition.

We look at the deeper principles of each therapy to learn more about how the mind and body work and how we can make more of our potential. Within our experience we have the aspects of Knower, Knowing and Known and therapies focus on these differently. Studying the different Doctor to Patient relationships also helps you see which therapy would suit you best. We also cover the evidence as to which therapies are shown to be effective.

There are main themes in overcoming depression across the mind, body and environment. Balance is fundamental to health in the physical body, in our activity and in our brain chemistry. Synchrony is the key to staying in tune with the physical environment. Connectedness with other people is a mainstay of emotional and social health. We need loving relationships and useful roles in society. In the mind we use our ability to transcend beneath the surface to reflect on our thoughts and feelings. Connectedness to the wider universe requires us to transcend to the deepest level of experience.

To avoid depression we need to keep on growing and achieving higher goals. Depression is never welcome but it can act as a prompt to look at our lives and not just at the more superficial parts of our thinking style and behaviour. It reminds us to reflect on our values and perspective at much deeper levels. To find bliss we must become truly mature and use all of our potential.

∞ Chapter 2 ∞
All Work and No Play
The Behavioral Approach

When we feel down our first reaction is to do something fun and enjoyable. Family and friends will give the same advice and hopefully take us out for a meal or to see an entertaining film. If this works then all is well and good but if we cannot enjoy ourselves then more thought is needed. An unfortunate symptom of more serious depression is the inability to find happiness in previously pleasing activity.

At a simple level we act to get reward or satisfaction just as a laboratory rat presses a lever to get food or navigates a maze to find cheese. Our rewards may be more sophisticated but the principles of Beahviorism are still very relevant to human life. Not enough rewards being achieved leads to dissatisfaction and depression.

The most obvious reason for insufficient rewards is not doing enough positive activities to gain satisfaction and happiness. There are several possible causes. Firstly you might just have the wrong balance of work and play. This supposes that your work is arduous or not very enjoyable. Or you may have other responsibilities which are draining. Of course there may be demanding circumstances such as financial hardship pushing you to working two jobs. For others of us we work too many hours unnecessarily. The extra money earned does not in fact improve our quality of life as we spend less time with family or at play. Rebalancing your activities involves either shifting some time from work to play, or changing your work so that this side of life becomes less stressful and more enjoyable, more meaningful.

Another explanation could be that you are not doing enough of anything. You have become lazy and just lie around watching TV all day. This could be a bad habit or you may have a physical problem lowering your energy. Possibly you have an impoverished environment where there is not much opportunity for play or creativity. Alternatively you may have already become depressed for some other reason and this has robbed you of motivation. You then do less and your depression worsens.

An opposite problem arises from too much activity. This can result from having too many commitments. If despite having two jobs you also keep up a high level of family life and play you become exhausted. Again balance is needed with regular rest at night, at weekends and in holidays being crucial for mental health.

There is a major difference between depression with low activation and depression with over-activity. In the first, the hypothalamic-pituitary-adrenal system is diminished. This is also seen in viral illness and Chronic Fatigue Syndrome. Arousal is low and sufferers feel sleepy. It is part of our immune and repair response to force extra rest on us. With over-activity this system is running too high producing over-arousal and less sleep. We become unable to relax until we are exhausted.

For some people too much activity is a life-style choice. This is common in a world where excitement is a major route to happiness. All night dance parties are fun but if they are frequent the mind and body cannot keep up. You can take drugs to keep you going but this only puts off the inevitable pay-back. If you are stressed by over-excitement you start to feel depressed when you are resting because you then realise how out of balance you are. Responding to this depression by forcing yourself into more excitement just leads to more damage. For our media stars who exemplify this life-style a period away from society in rehab has become a fashionable way to rebalance.

Doing wrong

Some activities cause direct harm. We do them because they also give some short term reward. Alcohol is a prime suspect with very quick relief of anxiety or forgetting why we are depressed. Longer term alcohol is a very depressing drug causing immense mental problems. There are others ways of impulsively reducing distress like smashing things or even people. You feel better for a very short time, and then you have to deal with regret and guilt. At the other end of this spectrum is harming your-self, for example by cutting. This may be the only way you can control your acute distress but it does not do much for your self-esteem. You need to learn healthier ways of coping.

As with doing too little, behaviour which causes harm can worsen depression. If you continue to deal with distress using the same harmful strategies your depression spirals down but it may not be easy to stop harmful behavior if it brings relief in the short term. New skills need to be learned and it is increasingly recognised that many of us lack basic skills such as coping with distress, problem solving, and communicating with others. These can easily and usefully be learned. The behavioral approach emphasises learning new positive behavior rather than focusing on why we are behaving negatively.

Karen and David were an apparently successful couple who had both become depressed. David ran a high-end food importing business which had made them wealthy, they had a beautiful home and they had a lovely young daughter. But they were both depressed. For Karen it was obvious that the ritzy home and motherhood were not enough even though she dearly loved her child. Karen's mother, sister and girl-friends all lived the other end of the country so she rarely saw them. David worked such long hours he was not at home much except to sleep. From David's side he saw creating wealth as an expression of his love for his wife and child.

David had reached a state of over-activity and was becoming exhausted. When not working he felt listless and not able to relax. At a basic behavioral level he needed less action and more rest. At another level he needed to re-evaluate his balance of activity, the work/life balance. The couple together were able to look at their goals and recognise that the pursuit money was being over-valued now that they were comfortably off. This involved a major change of gear for David which he did not find easy. The analysis behind this change was a very simple aligning of activity and goals. Both of them placed family life as their main priority but they were not putting their energy in the right direction to support this.

Karen's depression was one of under-activity. Despite having a young child, because Karen was very competent and organised and had no financial worries and her daughter was a calm healthy child, she did not find motherhood demanding. Family also meant to her, more than for David, a sense of extended family. To satisfy this she chose to spend more time with her distant family which did mean travel for them or for Karen but this was easily afforded.

The fact that two intelligent and successful people needed help to make such obvious changes shows how we can be stuck in behavioral patterns. David was trying harder and harder to feel better by gaining more financial success. The more tired he became the harder he worked to overcome this. Karen became stuck in inactivity and hopelessness feeling trapped. Her self-esteem and sense of direction had plummeted.

Cannot get satisfaction?

Sometimes depression strikes even though a person is neither over active, nor lazy, and is still doing things that used to make him happy. This occurs when the reward mechanism itself is damaged. Going to a new film with friends is just no fun anymore. This is a common experience and a significant sign in depression; the simple strategy of spending more time having fun has no effect. One misguided response to this is to try new activities to get satisfaction. Your marriage is no longer much fun so you have an extra-marital affair. You may blame your marriage for your depression. This could be a factor but if your depression and broken reward mechanism is the cause of your marriage problem, not vice versa, then looking for excitement in someone else's arms will be disastrous. Similarly you might blame your job and resign when it is the low mood that has made your work so boring.

The reward pathway in the brain is known and drug therapy for depression is one way of influencing this to restore the link between action and reward. Another way of looking at this is the cognitive approach. Thinking styles can undermine claiming your just rewards. If you attribute any bad outcome to being your fault and give credit to positive outcomes to chance or the environment then you rob yourself of deserved satisfaction. As we see in the next chapter there are other ways of weakening the link of activity to reward which can be remedied by changing your thinking.

Raising your sights

The last explanation at a behavioural level involves examining what your goals and values are. Activity leads to satisfaction but what is really satisfying to us? Yuppie syndrome or "affluenza" is a case in point. A man has strived to earn money and buy a beautiful apartment, car, gold watch, etc. He succeeds in this and becomes very wealthy. One day he wakes up and realises he is not as happy as he had hoped. He senses that earning even more money will not make him any happier. This is very disheartening as he has worked so hard and succeeded financially yet he feels unfulfilled.

During childhood it is natural to strive for different goals as we grow older. What interests and satisfies a 4 year old is of no interest to an 8 year old. This is obvious and natural. However once we reach adulthood we tend to stop looking for more mature goals and pursuits. Indeed many of the ideals and role models in our society reflect the desires of teenage not of adult life. Constant excitement, multiple partners, erratic sleep, bingeing on alcohol and drugs, and excessive concern with peers' opinion are understandable in our teenage years but we should be moving on to other goals in adulthood.

A rat may be content with a few stable activities: eating, sleeping, and playing with other rats. Higher animals have more complex desires with curiosity and the search for new activities being developed. Man has a huge range of roles available. We have a far higher potential and if this is not realised we become stale and bored if not frankly depressed. We need to allow our activities and rewards to evolve though life. This will include connectedness to others and being of use to others. We are social animals and we are spiritual beings. Religion is an uncertain part of many cultures now as religions themselves have not grown or evolved. When you have achieved the more basic goals in life you will find more satisfaction in developing the deeper social and spiritual aspects of life. This is especially true in older age when the end of your physical body is approaching. Our stages of development cannot be avoided by focusing only on the material and sensual levels of life.

Introducing Richard

Richard is an imaginary patient whom we shall send to see the different therapists described in this book. He is 28 years old and works as a teacher. He has a second episode of depression, the first occurring when he was 20 years old. This episode of depression has led to him struggling at work.

The first behavioral advice came from his girl-friend telling him he needed to take a holiday but he was unwilling to miss time at work during term. Richard did not think he was working too hard and he was concerned to stay in his job even though he had been finding it stressful. He wanted to tough it out till the school holidays.

He saw a Psychologist who first looked at a behavioural approach. He asked Richard to keep a brief diary of what he did and how his mood varied. In his week-days he would get back from work and eat quickly then go straight into paper work, correcting students' work or planning lessons. After this he relaxed watching TV till quite late. He did not get much joy from this but after a while he felt relaxed enough to go to bed. At the weekends he spent time with his girl-friend. Usually he would go to a bar in the evenings which he enjoyed. He did not feel so good the next morning with low motivation to do much.

Without going into why or how he arrived at this routine it was possible to suggest some simple changes. In the week he could find some relaxing activity to do after work before he did paperwork at home. Then he could find some alternative to TV which was more satisfying. In finding new behaviour he was encouraged to remember what had been enjoyable before and what his values and goals were. He identified just resting listening to music after work and reading historical fiction in the late evening. This was more satisfying as he thought of TV as a waste of time whereas reading had some aspect of improving himself.

At weekends he was asked to count his alcohol intake and look for other activities in the day. His girl-friend revealed she was concerned about his drinking and hang-overs prevented him being very human in the mornings. He agreed to cut down to one evening in the bar and decided to try to get more exercise. He saw fitness as desirable but hard to obtain. His girl-friend was a good model as she was a keen swimmer.

These changes did make a difference but he continued to find work arduous despite feeling somewhat brighter outside school. Examining his school work he found enjoyment in some lessons but found others stressful. He identified these classes as ones where he tended to lose control of the students and the lesson. He had blamed this on his own lack of character or energy. He was encouraged to find advice from a senior teacher he respected and arranged to have some mentoring. This amounted to him learning some new skills in classroom management.

The analysis and suggestions made may seem superficial but they allowed him to find activities which were more relaxing and enjoyable in the short term as well as being in better alignment with some of his deeper values. He used his own creativity to find the alternative activities and also identified someone from whom he could learn new strategies at work.

Behavior Therapy

BT is a brand leader in Anxiety disorders but is much less prominent than Cognitive Therapy in Depression. This is partly because informal behavioral advice is given to us by our friends and family if we have not already advised ourselves. Many doctors and therapists give some behavioural advice even if they are mainly prescribing medicines or using a talking therapy. It is often combined with Cognitive Therapy in Cognitive Behavioral Therapy, but this is mainly to back up the cognitive side rather than being a primary analysis of behaviour.

Behavior Activation Therapy has been growing in popularity recently. This formalises some of the principles described above. Types of activity are recorded and compared to mood in a diary. Activities are also analysed in relation to your goals, not just your feelings. This aligns your efforts with what is important to you in the longer term and at a deeper level. Such analysis also requires you to step back and go beyond the superficial attachment of activity to short-term rewards. As we see in the next chapter this stepping back to reflect on our behaviour and goals is itself a therapeutic process. The results of Behavioral Activation Therapy are to reduce avoidance of activity and increase confidence leading to more productive action. It leads to less time ruminating on depressive thoughts.

As we have seen there are several different possibilities as to how behaviour relates to depression and it is useful to know which is happening for you.

Balancing the Known

Behavior is a superficial part of life visible to our-selves and others. It is therefore part of the Known aspect of the mind which we seek to balance. The commonest form of therapy is informal with our friends. This commonly takes the form of modelling, to use Behavior Therapy language. Your friends go out for a run or a meal and invite you along. You simply have to go along and copy their behavior. There is nothing special here as this is a normal part of social life. No great analysis or profound thought is needed but retaining these normal outings is important to recovery from depression where social withdrawal is such a risk. The main benefits of BT come from just doing it. The body, part of the Known aspect of our life, is involved and the Knower and Known roles are not so important.

If you are reluctant your friends may encourage you to go along, to copy them, to remember that you feel better when active. If a therapist is involved they will further emphasise the learning aspect of restarting activity which requires some of your Knowing aspect. More formal therapy will also discuss the theory of BT requiring you to be in the Knower position as well. The useful support from friends has

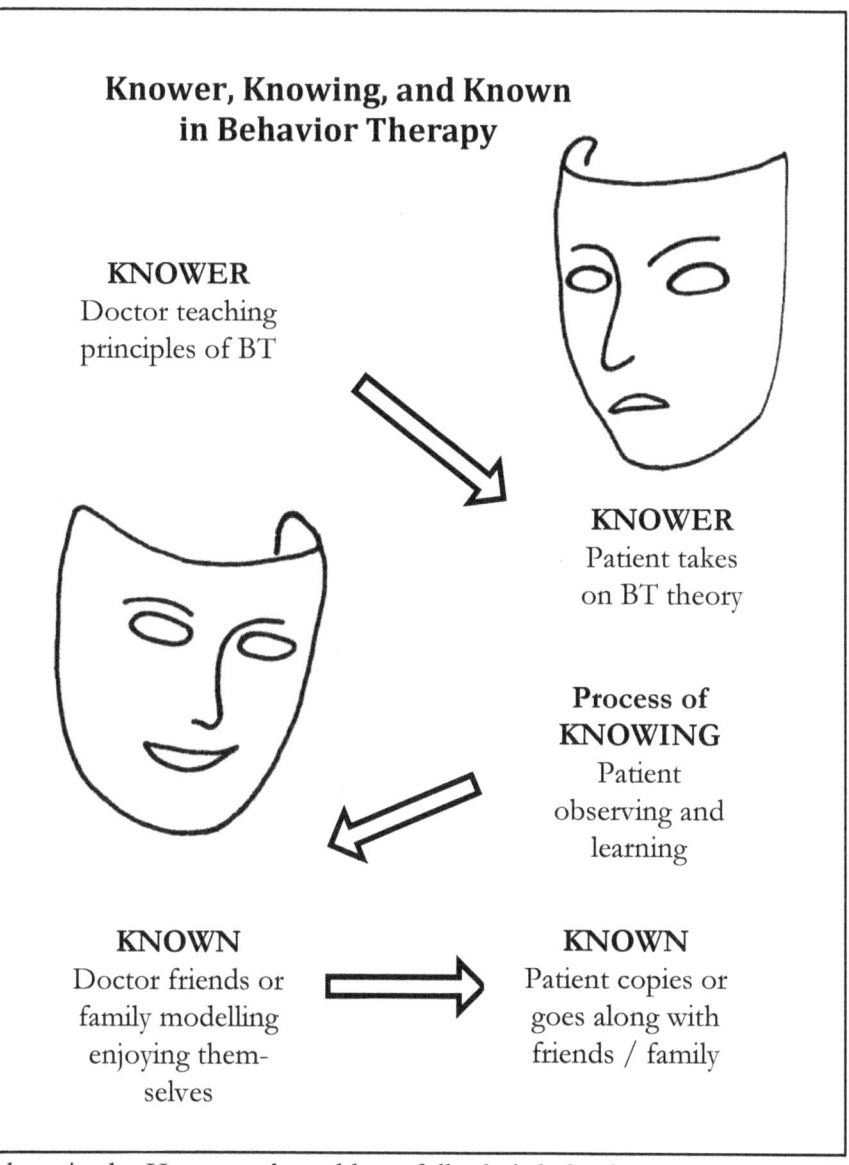

them in the Known role and hopefully their behavior encourages you to be active. Richard's girl-friend was a useful model for more exercise and less drinking. If she had also been stuck in inactivity and over indulgence of alcohol it would have been far harder for Richard to progress.

In more formal therapy such as Behavioral Activation Therapy there is more recording and analysis which use the "Process of Knowing" aspect of the mind. This analysis may initially be more in the mind of the therapist but the intention, as with many talking therapies, is to teach the patient to do the analysis for themselves. Depression is often a passive state and moving towards positive analysing, planning, and learning are important. These give enhancement of the Knowing and Knower roles. This is more prominent in Cognitive Therapy as we see in the next chapter but just stepping back to look at our behavior is a good step towards improving it. Taking ownership of knowledge is necessary if BT is to become part of the patient's future skill set.

Balance: simple but powerful

The behavioral level is often ignored as we assume depression is being driven by deeper levels of emotions or biochemistry and a depressed person may not be very motivated to change or do more. However we have seen that it is useful to understand behavior in quite simple ways. Are we too active or not doing enough? Is the balance of work, rest and play upset? Do our activities reflect our own values? Are there some harmful coping strategies holding us back?

BT is not concerned with the past or where depression came from. It is future and change oriented, optimistic and practical. It uses our natural supporters as co-therapists in helping us to recover. Behavioral advice can also be used as a part of therapy with other psycho-therapy or drug treatment alongside. Again this is often done without specifying the intervention as BT.

The one situation where this approach is not productive is when the reward mechanism itself is damaged, usually a sign of severe depression. Here another approach whether medication of psychological is needed at least initially.

There are some behaviors which are helpful not so much because they are immediately enjoyable but because they are healthy longer term. These include the changes to life-style recommended by Natural Medicine which we consider later. In a more enlightened state you naturally do enjoy healthy food but to a depressed carnivore an organic brown rice burger might not seem such a tasty idea.

Effectiveness of BT in Depression

Because BT is not much used in a formal way on its own there is little scientific evidence for its effectiveness. However it is so widely used informally and as a part of therapy that it is believed to be effective. Even where there is some clear cause for being depressed and some other specific treatment, keeping active can help you from sinking too low and speed your recovery.

As we shall see later there is growing interest in the relationship of depression and physical illnesses such as heart disease. Inactivity and lack of physical fitness are likely to be a common risk factor for both heart disease and depression.

Which people are suited to BT?

BT is simple and most people will have tried it to some extent themselves before consulting a doctor. For milder depression it may be enough to see you through. For more severe depression it is better used in conjunction with another approach and Cognitive Behaviour Therapy is a common choice. Because it is so simple it may be a main approach for individuals with dementia or intellectual handicap whose capacity for talking therapy is limited. It does not require either intellectual skill or emotional analysis. Paradoxically it may be useful for those with low motivation who are least likely to find it easy.

Behavioral advice is especially effective if your level of activity is too high, your coping methods are harmful, or you are working hard towards the wrong goals. If addiction or self-harm are part of your life then some behavioural analysis and advice aimed at these problems will be indicated. Redirecting the energy you already have should be possible.

BT looks to balance behaviour, which is a superficial Known aspect of mind, but it promotes the role of Knowing and learning to achieve this. It uses basic simple practical changes and encourages learning of new skills. These can combat helplessness and grow your confidence.

Summary

The behavioral approach is a powerful one not much used as a named therapy. We may have tried it informally ourselves or with friends and given up but it does deserve more attention. The basic strategies of balancing rest and activity, or work and play, are strong. We can check whether our activity is in line with our deeper values and whether our behavior needs to change to allow us to reach higher goals. We need to be very careful of coping strategies which cause more harm than good, such as alcohol.

We tend to think of depression in complex emotional terms or in terms of biochemistry. These approaches have their value but if simple advice around behaviour and balance is effective this may be easier and allow changes which actively promote your mental health.

Principles for a healthy mind identified in BT

- ∞ The mind naturally seeks happiness through activity
- ∞ A balance of different activities is needed for mental health
- ∞ A balance of rest and action is needed
- ∞ Growth and maturity guide more satisfying activities

Challenge for Behavior Therapy

For the friends and relatives of a depressed person the challenge is to stick with supporting them. Simple behavioral assistance is important and will be appreciated even if the immediate effect does not seem great. The challenge for highly trained therapists is not to over-look the obvious and jump to complex theories.

For society we need to recognise that our activity level is not just good for physical health but also essential for mental health and mood. We need both deep rest and dynamic action. Individuals and society find satisfaction from different activities as they mature through life which means challenging ourselves to find higher goals in life.

∞ Chapter 3 ∞
Seeing the Glass Half Full Cognitive Therapy

Our minds are always full of thoughts and when we are depressed these thoughts naturally tend to be sad ones. Does the depression come first or the negative thinking? It may not matter because once we are down this becomes a vicious circle with depressive thoughts lowering our mood leading to more depressive thinking. Cognitive Therapy (CT) looks to interrupt this cycle with more positive thinking.

As with Behavioural Therapy the initial cause of depression is less important than what is keeping you depressed. Compared to the more emotional psychotherapies this approach is straight-forward and reasonably brief. It can be learned from books to some extent or over the internet. CT is well proven as a therapy and there is evidence that the skills learned in CT can prevent future episodes of depression.

Thinking is a key human ability, especially the ability to think about our own thinking – reflective thought. We can infer that rats have some type of thought to mediate their complex behaviour but we do not see any evidence they reflect on their own thinking or create schools of philosophy. Even monkeys are not swinging through the trees chattering "I think therefore I am". The higher mental abilities characterise human life and give us great potential but they also bring vulnerability if these parts of the mind are not healthy. Mental illnesses seem much more evident in man than laboratory rats. CT uses some of these powers to strengthen the mind.

The most basic form of CT instructs us to reduce the number of negative thoughts and increase the number of positive ones. The next level is to look at our thinking patterns and modify these. Then there are specific skills that can be learned such as problem solving.

In any case the first step is to step back and reflect on your thoughts. As with the behavioural approach this first step in itself is helpful as it detaches you from being completely caught up in the negativity of your thoughts and so makes you feel less helpless. You start on a path to greater self-efficacy.

The next stage is to observe and record your thoughts, then you analyse them and see their pattern. Common patterns relate to our interpretation of events. Do we assume failure is our fault while attributing successes to others or to chance? Do you see the glass half full or half empty? Do we exaggerate any negative event or globalise it? Does one bad day at work mean all days will be bad? Does letting you partner down once mean you are always a terrible drag on the relationship?

CT deals with negative cognitions and these are presumed to relate to under-lying negative or dysfunctional beliefs about your-self, the world, and the future. When you are depressed your information processing is distorted so you see more of the down side of situations. These all make up another vicious circle with negative experiences reinforcing the depressive beliefs.

We then look at changing our thoughts and patterns of thinking. We can do this because they are all in our mind and by stepping back we can monitor and alter our thoughts. This is much easier than changing our emotions directly.

Once identified we either challenge or replace negative thoughts or put them in better perspective. As with anxiety, depression is accompanied by distortion of our thinking so we make more depressive interpretations. Looking at these in detail we can see these negative ideas as being unrealistic. We also seek to think more intelligently. Black and white thinking is a common problem with black being chosen more often than not in depression. A smarter approach is to see that there are shades of grey which protects us from extreme interpretations of events. We do not need to globalise minor disappointments in life.

Attention is another crucial factor in our experience. If I spend too long comparing my house and possessions with my rich neighbour's new toys then I feel not so good. If I think more of the many people less well off or my own past when I was less affluent, then I feel better about my situation. Remembering the half of the glass that is full counteracts unhelpful comparisons. Unfortunately our consumer society encourages negative comparisons to motivate us to buy more stuff.

Cognitive Behavioral Therapy

In practice cognitive methods are often supplemented by behavioural advice. New thoughts start manifesting as new speech and action — overt behavior. New behavior may be specifically advised to test out your new ability to interpret situations better. Putting thoughts into action strengthens them and gives you positive feedback. Hopefully others will respond well to your more positive presentation. You re-interpret a problem at work as not just being your fault. If you discuss this with a colleague or better your boss and they agree, this will be validating and uplifting.

There are a number of other brief therapies such as Interpersonal Therapy (IPT) which share the view that the cognitive, behavioral, emotional and interpersonal domains of life are related factors maintaining depression. They seek to change how we operate in these areas with cognitive and behavioral techniques.

Acceptance and Commitment Therapy (ACT)

This approach is predominantly cognitive though it has elements of Behavioral Therapy and Mindfulness. ACT takes a different approach to standard CT being less concerned with changing negative thoughts and thinking patterns. Instead it aims to reduce their impact and take away their power. ACT sees struggling against "symptoms" such as depressive thoughts as causing most of the distress in depression. If such thoughts are seen as transient and harmless in themselves we feel much less burdened. Acceptance that such thoughts occur but are no big deal is very beneficial.

To achieve this new perspective ACT uses a variety of cognitive techniques including use of paradox and metaphor to stir up new ways of looking at thoughts but the main strategy emphasises the importance of being able to step back from the superficial thinking level. Various mindfulness techniques are used such as being aware of the moment. ACT seeks to establish the "observing self", a deeper level of the mind which does not change. This provides a more stable element in the mind to help you cope with and dis-embed from the superficial changing level of depressing thoughts. This is a more Eastern approach to the mind which we discuss in greater depth later in this book.

The commitment side of ACT refers to an undertaking to find activity which is in line with your own values. This is the behavioral side which prompts you to do things which will be fulfilling at a more profound level. Hopefully these activities can replace those activities arising from depressive thinking, or just being inactive. This also increases your sense of self-worth and personal efficacy.

Both sides of ACT can be seen to use our attention, firstly to move attention away from the surface level of the mind and secondly to push it towards our own finer values to better motivate our actions.

There are other approaches which overlap with ACT such as Dialectic Behavior Therapy (DBT) which is targeted at Borderline Personality Disorder where depressed and varying mood are prominent. This uses more behavioural methods and mindfulness but CT elements as well. One skill specifically taught in DBT is distress tolerance. Severe distress may be so acute that it is hard to say if you are depressed, angry, frustrated or what. Another part of the training helps you to understand exactly what you are feeling.

Motivational interviewing is a scheme much used in addiction where intervention is tailored to the level of insight and readiness to change. Many of its techniques are cognitive such as using cognitive dissonance, for example recognising that what you say is important to you is not reflected in what you are doing.

Going beneath the surface - transcending

All forms of CT depend on the ability to step back and go to a deeper level of the mind. This is also called transcending the surface level. What do we find there? Firstly we can still think at the deeper level and these thoughts are more powerful as they exert influence over the more superficial level. We find the more "executive" functions of the mind such as monitoring, planning, and decision making.

The more profound levels are more intelligent and can correct the distortions of the surface thinking. They are also more positive as using more of our intelligence leads to a less depressive view of the world. More potential solutions are seen to problems facing us. More options are apparent. Complaints to your business become opportunities to improve and even a crisis becomes a time of great potential for positive change.

One explanation of why experiencing deeper levels is helpful is that they have this greater intelligence that allows us to see the world more positively. As we see in ACT another aspect of the deeper levels is the greater continuity or stability of experience. This is calm and reassuring in contrast to the changing level of distressing thoughts. Another factor is that inner more settled levels of the mind are also inherently more blissful, especially when we reach the deepest level of the mind – consciousness in its most settled state. However this level is very hard to reach by the intellectual skills of CT or by mindfulness techniques. For this reason a method to transcend to the deepest most blissful state of consciousness is useful.

Hypnosis

Hypnosis is another school of therapy which tries to get beyond the surface of the mind. There are many types ranging from the dramatic performance of putting people into a trance to the belief that hypnotic elements exist in normal conversation. Hypnosis can be used to suggest new ways of thinking and to aid you in recruiting your own imagination, but it is more suited to specific problems than general development of life. It is more effective if you have the ability to focus and to use imagination. Hypnotisability is a trait some people have making them much better subjects.

Hypnosis uses various tricks to get through the surface layer of the mind and intellect. The same techniques are seen in advertising and sales. Simple repetition is surprisingly effective. If I say something to you three times in a row it does sound more convincing. More cunning methods include nonsense statements which freeze the intellect to allow suggestions to slip through.

Dealing with disappointment

CT works best when your thinking is distorted and unrealistically negative. Unfortunately we sometimes experience events which are very disappointing or we just do not achieve our goals. A certain amount of reinterpretation or reframing may help and every cloud may have a silver lining. Even sour lemons can be used to make tasty lemonade but sometimes we are clearly not succeeding and feel bad about this. What does CT have to offer here?

Firstly we can analyse why we are not doing well. Have I been fired because I am useless or is it the global economy that is more to blame? We do not want to take more blame than is appropriate though it is worth recognising our own short-comings as we can then do something about them. CT does include particular skills such as problem solving. This is an ability which some people are much better at than others and it can be learned quite easily giving us more chance of finding a solution to a difficult situation.

Another level of analysis looks at what goals we are setting and then falling short of. Are we failing to meet our goals because they are unrealistic? Are we perhaps not setting clear goals so we have difficulty making progress in the right direction? If we do have clear goals, have we been monitoring our progress or do we only notice we are slipping when it is too late. Your marriage is very important to you but do you keep an eye on what you are contributing or do you take it for granted? When we build something physical we usually do have definite plans, time lines, checking procedures etc. However we often neglect such surveillance in less defined areas such as our career or family life. Much personal or life-coaching consists of applying this kind of analysis.

It is also possible that your goals are well planned and progress monitored but you have set the wrong type of goal. If you dedicate your time and effort to having many sexual partners you may well succeed but at some point this will no longer be so satisfying. You will need to move on to a more complete contact with partners. It is the nature of life to progress towards individual goals and our goals themselves need to evolve to higher levels.

Richard goes for Cognitive Therapy

The Cognitive Therapist starts off similarly to his behavioural colleague except that he concentrates on Richard's thoughts. A diary is kept and then patterns are identified. In practice there is some attention to behaviour as well if only to see in which situations different thoughts arise.

Richard's thinking is characterised by much self-blame and some black and white thinking. For example he sees his major problem in teaching one particular class as only reflecting on his poor teaching skills. He is asked to look more closely at this and he does discuss this with other teachers and finds that everyone finds this class quite hard work. This leads to a better interpretation of why the class is tough to teach and his previous negative attribution of blame to himself can be changed.

However this is not a black and white issue. It is not just one or the other: either he is to blame or the pupils are. At the same time as recognising that the class is hard for all teachers, Richard can recognise that he could do better. Although he already has some problem solving skills he has not tended to use them in this situation as he was lost in hopelessness. Refreshing his problem solving skills he identifies some things he already knows he could do differently in the class and also asks for some mentoring from the senior colleague. Admitting you need help is very different to being helpless. Maybe try telling that to a typical man who will not ask for directions when lost on the road.

When Richard is relaxing in front of the TV or in the bar he does not actually have very cheerful thoughts. He is distracted from negative thoughts but not usually experiencing happy thoughts. Cognitively he is successful in redirecting his thoughts from depressive ideas but not in finding happy thoughts. He identified that he needs to use more of his problem solving and creativity to find more rewarding activity. New activities would hopefully be more in tune with his deeper values or his goals in life. Richard wants to be a successful and respected man of knowledge and he wants to be a worthwhile man for his girl-friend to marry one day.

Richard benefitted from the CT approach. Firstly he stepped back to identify how many negative thoughts he had, then stepped further back to look at the type of thoughts and their validity. Then he transcended a bit more to reflect on his values and goals. This all led to some behavioral changes. He felt more confident about addressing his problems and was hopeful the skills he had learned would help him into the future.

Improving the Process of Knowing

CT is all about using more intelligence, the Process of Knowing. In Behavior Therapy the therapist or friend is in the position of the Known, to be observed. In CT the therapist is at least initially in the Knower position as a teacher. He then uses the patient's own Knowing ability to improve itself. He suggests patterns and provides feed-back.

As a patient you do have to act as observer of your own thoughts and you have to step back – altering your observation point, so the Knower aspect is also in evidence. The Known is your thoughts and patterns of thinking which are to be changed.

As therapy progresses the patient is expected to take more ownership of the knowledge and come up with more of their own improvements. This strengthens the Knower aspect of the mind and improves the Known – your thoughts themselves. But the main area of focus for CT is on the Process of Knowing.

CT underlines the value of mental discrimination so we can correct intellectual mistakes and achieve a more positive frame of mind. A healthy and intelligent mind will naturally support a more positive mood. Learning is again seen as central to health with the conscious mind expanding by increasing awareness of the

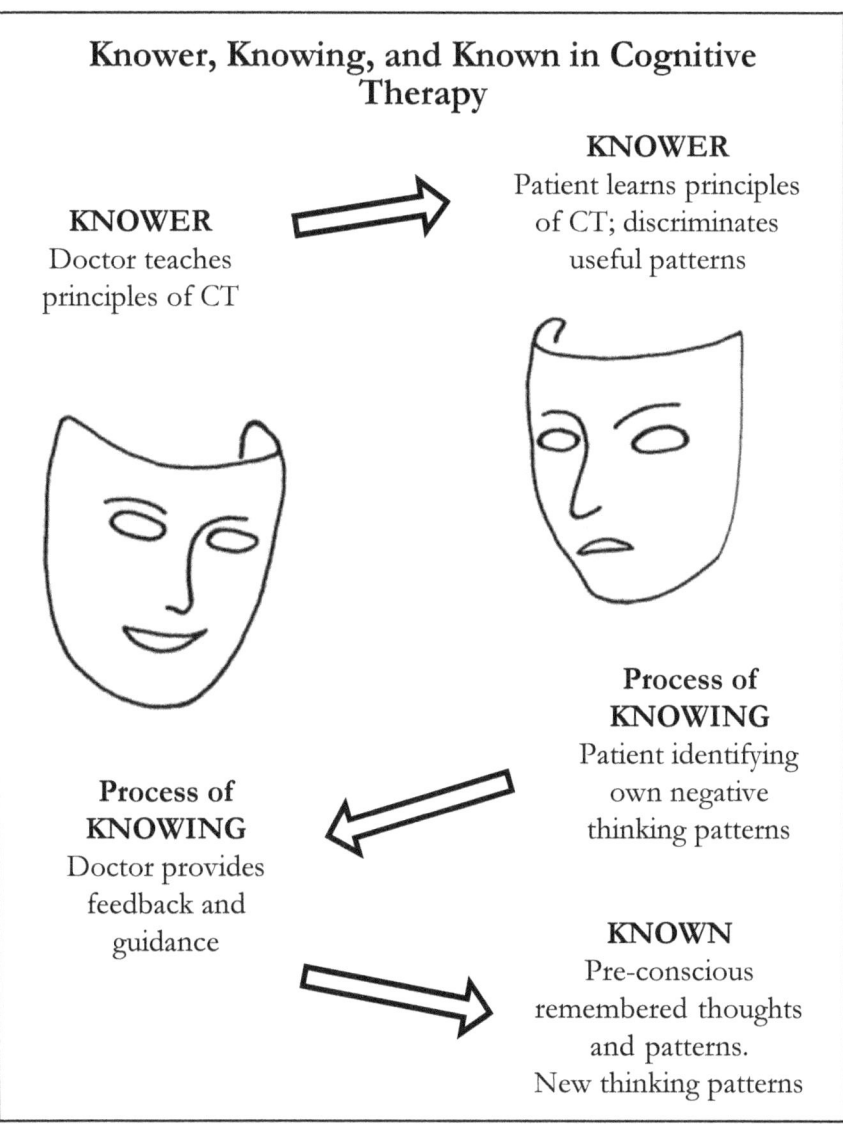

preconscious patterns and memories. A major difference from Psychoanalysis is that the significance and meaning of these preconscious tendencies is often insignificant. When the light of intelligent awareness is shone on them they disappear like shadows.

In order to examine and reprogram thinking patterns we make use of our ability to transcend to deeper level of the mind from where we can reflect on the more superficial levels. This is reflective thought or meta-cognition which is based on the fundamental characteristic of our consciousness - that it is aware of itself.

The cognitive path points directly towards the deeper levels of the mind though does not reach the deepest, Transcendental Consciousness. From deeper levels the more superficial areas of the mind can be reflected on and restructured. From the most settled state of intelligence, we avoid mistakes and a positive frame of mind can be maintained in any situation. CT is itself still evolving. Some of its ideas are coming close to Buddhism, that most cognitive of religions. This is the closest link so far between a mainstream therapy and a philosophy acknowledging clearly the value of transcendental states.

Evidence for CT in Depression

Cognitive Therapy has strong evidence to support it. It is as effective as anti-depressant medication for mild and moderate depressions. It used to be advised that it is not so useful in severe depression but studies suggest it is effective but needs to be more intensive and go on for longer than the usual eight weeks.

One of the most encouraging findings has been that after a course of CT you are less likely to relapse into a further episode. A landmark NIMH study showed relapse down to a third at one year compared to anti-depressants. For anti-depressant drugs there is no protection from relapse once you stop the medication. When CT works it leaves some lasting change in your thinking patterns or beliefs.

For chronic or persistent depression the results for all therapies are worse than for short-lived episodes, not surprisingly. The combination of CT and anti-depressants does better than either alone. There is some evidence for CT being especially useful in people with histories of childhood abuse or neglect when compared to medication.

CT can be applied in the purely cognitive realm but it is more common for some elements of Behavior Therapy to be included which makes it CBT. Much of the evidence concerns this mixed model. Testing out your new thinking in different situations serves to validate and reinforce progress. Knowledge and experience complement each other

Which people are comfortable with CT?

CT does not require a high level of intelligence but is easier for people used to abstract thinking. However developing the habit of abstract thought is also very useful for people who do not usually use this ability. CT is very rewarding if you tend towards helplessness and lack of the Knower role. Obviously CT is a good choice if you are already aware of being stuck in bad thinking patterns. CT is a positive approach and does not typically involve going over past traumas and negative experiences so it would appeal to you if you want to look forward rather than looking back to sort out the past.

Cost is an issue as is availability of therapists both of which support the growth of on-line delivery of CT. Another factor is how comfortable your referring doctor is with CT. Many will go for the combined approach of drugs and CT (or CBT) but if your depression is not severe you could consider just trying the CT first. For children and teen-agers the evidence is more positive for CBT and drugs have become much less recommended.

Summary

Cognitive Therapy is the leading psychological therapy for depression today. It is well evidenced and has a clear program of work. CT uses our unique human ability to reflect on our own thinking to transcend beyond the surface of the mind. We step back and examine our Process of Knowing. Improving our thoughts leads to better mood. We can also improve our problem solving and learn other specific skills.

Principles for a healthy mind identified in CT
- ∞ The mind has abstract levels below the surface thinking level
- ∞ Our attention can easily transcend to these deeper levels
- ∞ Deeper levels are more intelligent
- ∞ Deeper levels support confident positive mood
- ∞ Knowledge and experience support each other

Challenge for Cognitive Therapy

Cognitive Therapy is becoming more widespread in its application outside of therapy into business development, sports, and personal life coaching. It could be more usefully deployed in schools to ensure young people have the basic thinking skills they need and in many countries this is starting to happen.

Another challenge for CT is to keep going to deeper levels. There is more connection being made with the emotional theories in terms of working with complexes or schemes in the mind which incorporate both thinking patterns and emotional problems. More interesting would be for CT to keep transcending down into the simplest state of consciousness which has no specific content. CT recognises that stepping back is an essential and natural ability. It has yet to see its way down to transcending all relative thought as being equally natural and useful.

∞ Chapter 4 ∞
Separation and Loss
Psychoanalytic Therapies

Psychoanalysis has been very influential in shaping our ideas about the mind especially regarding our emotions. It has a good deal to say about depression but much of this is pessimistic. Freudian analysis was the foundation method developed around the start of the twentieth century. Since then many schools have evolved, a dozen well-known and many dozen less celebrated. It was the dominant school of thought mid-twentieth century but has fallen from its pedestal since then. However it still has much to teach us.

When Freud was formulating his ideas in Europe there were some very negative philosophies around. Human life did not seem to be ideal despite the great political revolutions, industrial progress, and more individual freedom. Today we have the even greater joys of the electronic age to entertain us yet depression is now more common.

Freud wanted to discover the motivations and drivers within the mind causing depression and other mental illness. He used a scientific approach to his research applying some of the ideas of chemistry and physics to parts of the mind. He looked at the mechanics within the mind for drives and resistances and for separate objects interacting. One of his general discoveries was the tension between our more basic animal drives and desires, such as aggression and the sex drive, and the constraints of society with its conventions and laws. The individual ego struggles to negotiate between these two poles so it is not surprising therefore that we fail to feel satisfied and depression is almost to be expected.

This challenge is most evident in our problems with sexual relationships. The basic drive has won out over the social constraints in many societies giving us much more sexual freedom but sexual problems are still widespread as any women's magazine will tell you. Perhaps it is the other levels of our intimate relationships which are not being fulfilled and sex cannot be separated out from these. Freud wrestled with these problems but he was more concerned with negative sides of life than positive. Uncomplicated love, trust, altruism and especially spirituality did not fit so well into his scheme. We do have to mesh our individual desires with the greater needs of society but this should not be so hard. Many of the most respected people are those who do manage this and clearly enjoy themselves in the process.

Worshipping independence

In modern times we have seen family size decrease dramatically and people are more mobile geographically. The stable back-ground of the church is less visible and no longer do we assume our lives will be like our parents'. We see independence or self-sufficiency as being an essential part of maturity and mental health. In some ways they are features of being a successful grown-up but we also find that connectedness with other people is a prime protector against depression and crucial to having a fulfilling life. It is natural to become somewhat independent of your original family and then start your own intimate relationships and form a new family but how independent do we need to be? Psychoanalysis has been one cause of us expecting to be extremely independent. Now we all have to discover our own ideas, desires, morals, and way of living. We must find our self or feel imprisoned in the fetters of social expectation. This is a hard task for many and can feel like everyone having to re-invent the wheel.

In some ways we are more connected than ever. Who does not have hundreds of friends in social media sites? But connections are often superficial or distant. A real geek is unsure even of the actual gender of his closest friends as he has never met them in person. We have yet to come to terms with electronic relationships but the increased connectivity has fantastic promise. In the transitional time we live in there is high risk of the electronic world distracting us from the more immediate relationships in our lives. The internet is high on imagery and quick excitement but low on human warmth and peacefulness. Having a hundred TV channels does not reduce loneliness, the common companion of depression.

Separation and loss

The flip side to independence is separation from other people. This can occur through growing up and leaving home or through the death of close friends and relatives. Lesser losses occur through breaking up with partners or just moving location. This theme of separation and loss is a major facet of Analysis. Some of the derivative schools make this their main focus.

Loss in adult life is common as people die or move away or situations change. Separation from our parents is more complicated with various stages of increasing autonomy between infancy and adolescence. We feel sad when we learn that our mother is not all-powerful and able to satisfy our every need. We feel sad when we separate from the close intimacy of infancy. Can we come to terms with this? Can we accept the imperfections of the world and feel secure in our own independence? When these stages go wrong the mind sets up abnormal or distorted patterns of feelings and relationships.

If you are unfortunate and lose a parent in childhood it is more likely you will experience depression as an adult. Death of any loved one even from natural causes is still a potent cause of distress and depression. Grief is expressed differently across cultures with sadness and some pain being common and accepted as natural. When suffering goes beyond the normal for your culture you may have drifted from normal grief to depression. This is more likely if you are prone to depression or if the loved one was someone you were dependent on or if the death was unexpected or unnatural.

It is interesting that there is so much literature on the grieving process – how we who are left behind deal with death. This process is generally well agreed on with specific stages to go through. In contrast the harder question of what has actually happened to the person who died is not addressed by psychotherapy because it is seen as the province of religion and we do not all agree in this realm.

There is a danger of psychology and psychiatry taking over death, just as hospital medicine has taken over birth, even though they cannot answer this most important question.

Handling failure

Death of a partner may be the most potent stress but often depression follows lesser set-backs. How do we understand the dynamics here? There is no doubt that disappointment or failure can lead to feeling down but some disappointments are inevitable in life, just as growing out of childhood is inevitable. How do we deal with facing up to imperfections in life? One useful concept is that of the "good enough mother". We recognize that our mother is not all-powerful and able to satisfy our every desire immediately but at the same time we know that she is good enough to nurture us and support us towards a healthy life. In fact having some disappointments is necessary to stimulate resilience in a child. If childhood is too perfect we may not learn the strengths we need to survive adult life. There is an on-going debate in schools as to whether children should be protected from losing, in sports for example, leading to very non-competitive activity. Should children be praised no matter what they do or will this lead to them becoming fragile narcissists?

As adults we do live in a very competitive society. Even on TV most "reality" shows revolve around competition and judgement. Some competition can be managed by being clear what your goals and values are. Do you really want to be a better cook than other people? Perhaps being a good enough cook is a better goal. You then also stand more chance of enjoying other peoples' cooking successes. It is also best to know when you have succeeded at one level and can move on to a new higher goal.

In adult life we need to be able to deal with everyday let-downs and more distressing losses. CT can help through reframing and helping us see positives but this is not always appropriate. If your wife of many years dies you probably do not want to start reframing this too soon as an opportunity to see other women. If you have made major mistakes in life, such as harming your family through your alcoholism, it may be very hard to move on from feelings of guilt and depression. For some, the church has had a role here, both in dealing with grief for the death of loved ones and in the area of forgiveness.

In the Psychoanalytic method a direct opportunity for dealing with loss comes with the ending of therapy and for some patients this will be the most important phase. You have the chance to leave your therapist in a constructive and positive manner allowing you to remember what you have learned and accept you can cope without him or her. This could be a very different experience to previous losses which perhaps left you with anger or remorse or overwhelming sadness. Similarly within the therapy you can learn that while the therapeutic relationship is intimate and special neither you nor the therapist are perfect and some stresses arise which can be usefully worked through.

An unusual solution

Christine was a lady in her early 70's who had lost her husband of many years to a sudden illness. This was a devastating blow to her as she had few friends or family. She regarded her long marriage as a bit of a miracle as she was generally critical of other people. Her husband had crept under her defences but had not been able to change her attitude to others. Possibly this related to her upbringing which was emotionally harsh. Without her husband she became extremely lonely and depressed. She was encouraged to get out more but she resisted due to her distrust of others and also her arthritis and poor mobility.

After a year her doctor thought that enough time had been allowed for grieving and she was persuaded to take anti-depressants. These had little effects and she did not like drugs anyway. A kindly psychologist visited her but she was suspicious and did not reveal much to her even though the psychologist had gone the extra mile and seen her at home. She did not try other therapies but one of her few acquaintances told her to get a computer and see if she could find something to interest her on-line. Surprisingly she took this advice. The infinite variety of the internet means there really is something for everybody. Through random searching around she hit on some sites concerned with conspiracy theories. These were a lifeline to her. She joined a community of people, none of whom she had to meet and became quite an expert on some very odd ideas. Her mood improved greatly.

I probably would not have advised her as a person already prone to paranoid ideas to seek out activity related to themes of distrusting the government and cover-ups. However for her this was just the right balance of contact with others and her psychological set. She did not unearth and understand her reasons for being distrustful but we could say her ego found a way to satisfy these tendencies while also having enough human contact and interest in life to remain happy.

The process of therapy

Psychoanalysis and its offshoots are sometimes called process therapies because it is the process of therapy that is most important, not the content. This process is not straight-forward, as it is in BT and CT, because in the analytic therapies we are trying to learn about the unconscious which is not easy to bring into our conscious waking mind. You might be apparently happily married and see nothing wrong with your spouse but thinking about your marriage somehow makes you feel depressed. Perhaps your unconscious is holding a very different fantasy of what your husband should be like and while your conscious mind has compromised and enjoyed him for what he is, your unconscious has not given up its ideal image and is disappointed in him. Or maybe your unconscious has picked up the subtle signs that he is not that happy and may be having an affair while your conscious mind does not want to see this. Or there may be unresolved feelings about your parents which are clogging the unconscious up.

One of the main avenues for therapy is in the therapeutic relationship. This is important in any therapy but in analytic therapies it is absolutely crucial. The unconscious patterns of your relationships in life will be played out in the relationship with your therapist. This is referred to as the "transference" of unconscious feelings from another, usually past, relationship into therapy. Analysing this transference is the principal form of therapy in many schools. Alongside this is the analyst's "counter-transference' which contains transference of their own past, plus reaction to the therapy relationship. Counter-transference is potentially most useful as it can allow the analyst to directly experience some of the patient's feelings. These feelings can include early pre-verbal experiences which cannot be recounted easily and severe trauma experiences which are also be hard to express in words.

Transference and counter-transference explain why analysts need to be analysed them-selves so they are not bringing too much of their own problems into the therapy. It also explains why Freud recommended analysts reveal nothing about them-selves, even to the point of sitting behind the patient lying on the couch so they are not in direct view. This is intended to make it easier for the patient to project whatever they want onto the blank screen of the analyst's personality. If you are angry with your therapist for being late or missing a session this may be quite reasonable at a superficial level but it can also relate to your anger at some-one in the past such as a father who did not give you enough time and attention. Not getting attention led to your having low self-esteem and depression. It is probably too late to process your early childhood with your father, especially if he still does not give you enough attention. You can recognise this happening in therapy and understand it and then put it in its place in the past rather than letting it overshadow the present.

This may all seem rather strange and many modern therapies expect a more equal interaction with the doctor revealing more about him or her-self. It also takes a very long time to achieve results with Freud's original method. Almost all modern therapies are much briefer and would be called psycho-analytic therapies rather than pure Psychoanalysis.

Another way of looking at the mind is to see it as fragmented and complex with health coming from more integration. One of Freud's great achievements was to describe the mind as having many inter-acting parts. Even if we do not all agree with his exact picture the general idea has great value. Once unconscious feelings or fantasies have been unearthed we can then integrate them with our conscious ideas and feelings. You might not have lived up to the unconscious dream of marrying an Olympic athlete but you might persuade your partner that you could both get fitter. Your fantasy job that you cannot possibly do may be attainable in another form as a leisure activity. Most men do not become star football players but this does not usually lead to depression. They can enjoy watching, playing at an amateur level or becoming part of a football club in another capacity.

Looking at the parts

"Object relations" therapies put our relationships at the centre of therapy. How we experienced our early life and coped with separations are crucial. If we develop feelings that are not well integrated we are likely to struggle with our adult feelings towards others and towards our-self. It is seen as normal to have positive and negative feelings about one's mother in childhood. Usually we can accommodate these different views and reach a more mature view of a mother who is positive but not perfect. If we do not then the positive and negative feelings will not lie easily together and this leads to new problems. For example, I deal with the opposites by holding on to a purely positive view of my mother and take the negative aspects into my view of myself. I take the blame for disappointments in life and end up with poor self-esteem and depression. Or I could project bad feelings out onto other people and become paranoid.

Child abuse is a particularly hard and nasty relationship dysfunction commonly leading to depression. If you are abused you may be confused by a parent who cares for you and also harms you. This confusion is carried into your adult relationships. Domestic violence is another toxic experience as is persistent bullying. In these situations you are being hurt by someone who is hard to get away from and who may also be your source of support or care. You can lose your sense of self-esteem and self-worth making it even harder to survive on your own so making escape more difficult. You lose trust in others, who have failed to protect you, and blame yourself. This is an "I am not OK" and "You are not OK either" position.

You are dependent on the opinions of others even though you do not trust them. Obviously the best answer is to prevent such abuse or bullying occurring in the first place. Tragically it often recycles with people who have been harmed in this way then harming others.

Freud's insight was that our external relationships were reflected in our internal dynamics. We carry these inner patterns with us even though the initial problem or people may have long gone. If our inner workings could be analysed and sorted out then our external world would have a chance to improve. Integrating and making connections among parts of our own mind leads to better connectedness in the social world outside.

Self-knowledge

Another analytic idea is that of the imagined, ideal, or fantasy image we have of ourselves. Some of this is conscious, like wanting a promotion at work, and some unconscious, like perhaps desiring a very different job for which you are not qualified at all. It is normal and good to have some more positive dreams to work towards. However if these fantasies are too far from reality they can lead to a sense of failure and frustration. Some psychotherapies emphasize the handling of this tension between the self and the idealized self.

If our actual self as we experience it consciously is too far from the unconscious ideal or fantasy self we shall feel uncomfortable. If we are falling well short then depression may result. Somewhere in your unconscious may be the goals that you expect to achieve by the time you are forty. When the magic age arrives and you have not achieved a beach house and a Mercedes or run a marathon, then the unconscious disappointment can make itself felt. Some of the goals could be well known to your conscious mind and not be concealed. What if you had some less acceptable expectations like having an extra-marital affair or killing that guy who bullied you? The mind might keep these in the cellar making the cause of your depression unknown.

Freud identified the individual ego as being vulnerable as it had to compromise between the primitive desires of the mind and the restrictions of external reality. Some schools of therapy concentrate

Psychoanalytic Therapies

their analysis on the ego and try to strengthen it. Different schools of therapy have their views on whether the ego has its own place and identity in the mind or if it is formed only from the conflicts between drives and restrictions. Freud described the ego as a rider on the horse of unconscious urges, but he was unsure how much authority the ego had to provide direction.

Later therapists such as Erikson saw the ego as having a much more positive role in developing a sense of identity, purpose and direction in life. He also described its phases of development. In early childhood we need to develop autonomy. If this is squashed by excessive criticism we grow up with low self-esteem. In adult life we must balance independence with forming new intimate sharing relationships without which we feel isolated. Failure to graduate successfully through the phases of development can lead to emotional problems. Poor self-esteem or feeling isolated and lonely can lead to depression. Lack of purpose and identity are also risk ingredients for depression and the term "identity crisis" entered our dictionary.

We live in an age that celebrates the individual and this pushes us to try to feel unique and special which would be fine if it were not for the fact that we are also quite alike and most of us are not world champions at anything. Intimate and loving relationships do fill this gap to an extent. You are the most special person to your spouse. Every baby is the most wonderful to their parents. But there is also great value in gaining identity, purpose and worth from a larger self and this is can be found in two ways.

Firstly there is belonging to a group of people whether family, tribe, religion, nation, or football team. We gain the strength of our team-mates and celebrate our collective success. This sort of larger self is very evident in collectivist cultures where it may be overt that the family or tribal group is the main event and individual desires are secondary. The individual has to serve the group. In such cultures, to generalize, individual mood is given less value and the integrity, achievement and reputation of the group are of more importance. This can protect against depression as you can enjoy the well-being of the group even when you are not in great shape as an individual.

However you may have difficulty surviving outside the group as you do not have such strong autonomy and individual self-esteem. Worst of all is when the group is abusing you as you then feel bad within the family but do not have the strength to leave it. You may be persuaded that it is your fault just to compound your problem. Collectivist cultures tend to have more defined family roles and as such can be less open to discussion about relationships. Psychoanalysis is a very individual pursuit and starting the journey of analysis from a collectivist back-ground can be challenging.

While Freud stressed the difficulty an individual has in accepting the restrictions of society, his modern descendants, such as the Humanists, take a more optimistic view. Other people and relationships are seen more as potential supports than as sources of conflicts. Depression is commoner if you are not connected to others so connectivity is seen as positive. The development of group therapy, discussed in a later chapter, has also shown the value of group consciousness. Humanists are also more optimistic about the deeper areas of the psyche which are found to have creative potential rather than being dominated by dark forces.

Spirituality

The second approach to finding an expanded self is to go within your-self to the areas beyond the level of superficial differences. Spirituality was not a part of life dealt with well by Freud. Jung had more interest and saw spiritual problems as a common feature of depression especially in later life when the question of mortality is looming. Later in the 20th Century more types of therapy have seen spirituality not just as a relevant part of mental life but as the whole basis of experience. These include the Trans-personal schools. Most theorists agree that the answers to the important spiritual challenges are not intellectual or simple emotional changes. They require some experience of the deeper self and the transcendental level of life. Traditionally religion is another source of answers with some religions emphasizing such direct experience and others more reliant on the teaching of their scriptures.

Depression may be due to a lack of spiritual awareness or a lack of meaning in life. Such depression can have a different quality, that of existential despair. You might look OK on the outside and even seem to be enjoying life but inside you feel nothing is worthwhile. One variant of this is found in people who have had brief glimpses of a higher state of consciousness and been unable to regain it. Their "normal" state of mind seems dull in comparison. We also see this is artists who have lost contact with their muse and inspiration.

Another brand of inner emptiness occurs in Borderline Personality Disorder which is a developing epidemic of our age. The heart just seems empty or "comfortably numb" as Pink Floyd sang. Having no emotion is more comfortable than the distress and turmoil of engaging in emotional life. This experience does not fit so well into Freud's dynamic view of the mind and in recent times practices of meditation or mindfulness have become main-stream in therapy. These are discussed more in later chapters.

The Unconscious

Psychoanalysis is much concerned with history. What happens in childhood has great effects on your adult emotions and relationships. This memory is largely unconscious so the problems you are carrying around with you are not as easily discovered as for example the negative thinking patterns found in Cognitive Therapy. Not only are the problems and conflicts buried in the unconscious they can actively resist being dug up. This is because they are too embarrassing or otherwise unacceptable to the conscious mind and they do not easily fit in to our external reality and conscious self-image. This resistance or defence has its own purpose. Suppose your inner desires are extremely aggressive, then keeping a lid on these could prevent you from assaulting people and being arrested. However if these urges then find an outlet in you harming yourself, you suffer depression and may be confused as to why this is happening. Such a scenario can result from prior abuse when you blamed yourself for being abused in order to retain a positive image of the abuser who was also your carer. Digging up this material would not be pleasant but it could enable you to sort out these confused feelings and move on.

Freud was fascinated by the question of how to know the unconscious which by definition is not immediately available to us. In the process of Analysis you as the patient discover that unconscious country with the Analyst as your guide. Dreams, whether nocturnal or day dreams, are big signposts on your journey within. Other directions come from looking at your own emotions and relationships and finding areas that make no obvious sense. You have a great husband in every way but you no longer find him attractive. In the unconscious there may be a clear reason.

Exactly how the unconscious mind is arranged is disputed. Jung described us as having complicated unconscious personalities including one of the opposite gender. He also mapped out a number of archetypes or common dynamic patterns that are found. Once unconscious material is discovered and made available to your conscious mind it is not just disarmed and discarded like an unexploded mine. It may be usefully integrated into your conscious personality. This allows expansion of the mind to occur. Even opposing tendencies can be integrated or synthesised to give a more mature and sophisticated mental landscape. You then have a greater range of roles and responses available to you.

Collective consciousness

Just as the individual mind has an unconscious area, so does the collective consciousness. Indeed Jung proposed that we are not so aware of collective consciousness because so much of it is unconscious. He found similarities between the stories and characters in mythology and folk-lore and the workings of the collective unconscious. These stories and roles exist through time and often across cultures. Many cultural arts and traditions can be seen as informing us about the collective mind of our tribe or nation.

The existence of a collective mind is challenging to our individualist psychology partly because modern science does not understand consciousness at all well even for an individual. If we look to the deeper explanations of the material world such as quantum field theory, we find that individual sub-atomic particles are manifestations of a wider underlying field. It would be surprising if individual consciousness did not have at least as subtle a relationship with others.

If you are depressed as a single person potentially the cause could be in the group consciousness. We see this at an obvious level when there is economic stress or political oppression causing many individuals to be stressed or depressed. Religions also play a role with different religious affiliations being a major predictor of suicide rates. More difficult to see are the other conflicts and frustrations in collective consciousness. Is there a collective shame about past wars or political abuses? Does your ambivalence about sexual life reflect not a specific problem in your relationships but a society level issue, still affecting your individual experience?

A simple pragmatic piece of advice is to put your problems in the context of your culture and its history. This may be protective of too much blame or pain being focussed on you and allow some higher level answers to emerge. For example if you have suffered loss and trauma and depression due to political or economic changes, understanding these can reduce your individual guilt. You remain responsible for doing what you can to improve your situation but knowing the restrictions under which you operate can be helpful. Seeking to change the circumstances through joining a political party or a pressure group will make you feel less helpless.

Jung's detailing of archetypes offers us the possibility of using or summoning different aspects of our unconscious. The Warrior strives to achieve through effort and bravery and fighting. When this approach is failing you could look at some others. Do those around you need more of the Care-giver or Lover from you? Is more creativity required from the Creator or Magician? These patterns of behavior or personalities can be found in you. You may find them being prompted in your dreams or the films you choose to watch.

The transcendental side to life

Analytic schools tend to see the conscious self as one part of the mind. Deeper levels of the mind seem dangerous territory for this small self to venture into, like an explorer going alone into a wild jungle. The Humanist therapists are more optimistic that our self can grow. As we discover and integrate more of the unconscious mind, our conscious awareness expands becoming deeper and stronger. As we achieve emotional and psychological growth we can move to higher levels of achievement. Different schools see growth in different areas being desirable.

Maslow described levels of achievement starting with the basics of shelter and food and leading up to self-realization. Cloninger has also described a healthy personality as having not just Self-directedness but then Cooperativeness and Transcendence being able to relate to the wider cosmos. This takes connectedness with others to the next level. An analytic perspective would be that by connecting and integrating all the parts of mental life we achieve a greater wholeness of experience. This is reflected in our relationships with others and becomes a reciprocal process.

One question not answered by Analysis is: "What is the medium in which all the parts of experience are found?" It is clearly some form of consciousness. If we take a parallel approach to that of quantum field theory then consciousness is an underlying field in which there are different patterns of excitation or activity. These appear as different people or different parts of the mind in one person. As our experience becomes expanded and integrated we become aware of more of these parts and their collective wholeness but there is also the potential to experience the field itself. This is a transcendental experience as the field itself lies beyond any specific part. At the same time the field pervades every part so we can also see that infinite value in a particular experience or a particular person. This is felt as love and as a deep sense of meaning and connectedness. Some modern offshoots of analysis go towards this goal but Freud would probably not have approved as he was suspicious of finding too much positivity when looking inwards.

Richard in Analytic Therapy

Richard's experience in process psychotherapy would be very different to BT or CBT. He is only in a position to have weekly therapy and even this is not easy to fit into full-time work. As a student of history he is attracted to a therapy that seeks to understand his own past. He is aware that something is out of balance in his life. He feels he is on the way to becoming what he wants to be, a respected teacher and a worthy husband, but is unsure how to make more progress.

The therapist does not suggest any starting point and Richard chooses to begin with this sense of knowing what he wants to be and not being able to achieve it. His parents are soon mentioned as important figures. They have always been supportive of his desire to be a teacher and generally approve of his girl-friend but they have never been very rewarding, especially his father. Richard is ambivalent about his father as he does want his approval but at the same time does not really respect him, particularly his drinking which is excessive. There is an obvious link here to Richard's own drinking. These themes take some weeks to work through but allow Richard to separate out some of the positive things he has inherited or learned from his father from the less desirable which do not fit into his own values and plans. Being surer in his own ability allows him to make better use of the more senior staff. His ambivalence towards his father had muddied these work relationships.

The therapy does not have a distinct end. Does he want to spend more time analysing his relationship with his girl-friend? This might be useful but as their relationship is fairly good maybe it is OK to let this evolve on its own.

Becoming the Knower

Analytic therapy wants to put the patient in the Knower position to know him or her-self but the journey is complicated. The doctor here is a guide into the territory of previously unknown areas of the mind. The Known that you need to find in analysis is initially unconscious, hence the unusual and indirect methods. This is a long way from simply keeping a diary of behaviors or thoughts, though a dream diary is part of some practices. More of the work occurs in the sessions themselves and in the therapeutic relationship. Within the transference relationship the role of your doctor may change to represent different people in your past or even parts of yourself. The overall role of the doctor here is to be the Process of Knowing. He does not come out with answers but provides a therapeutic space in which you can find these your self.

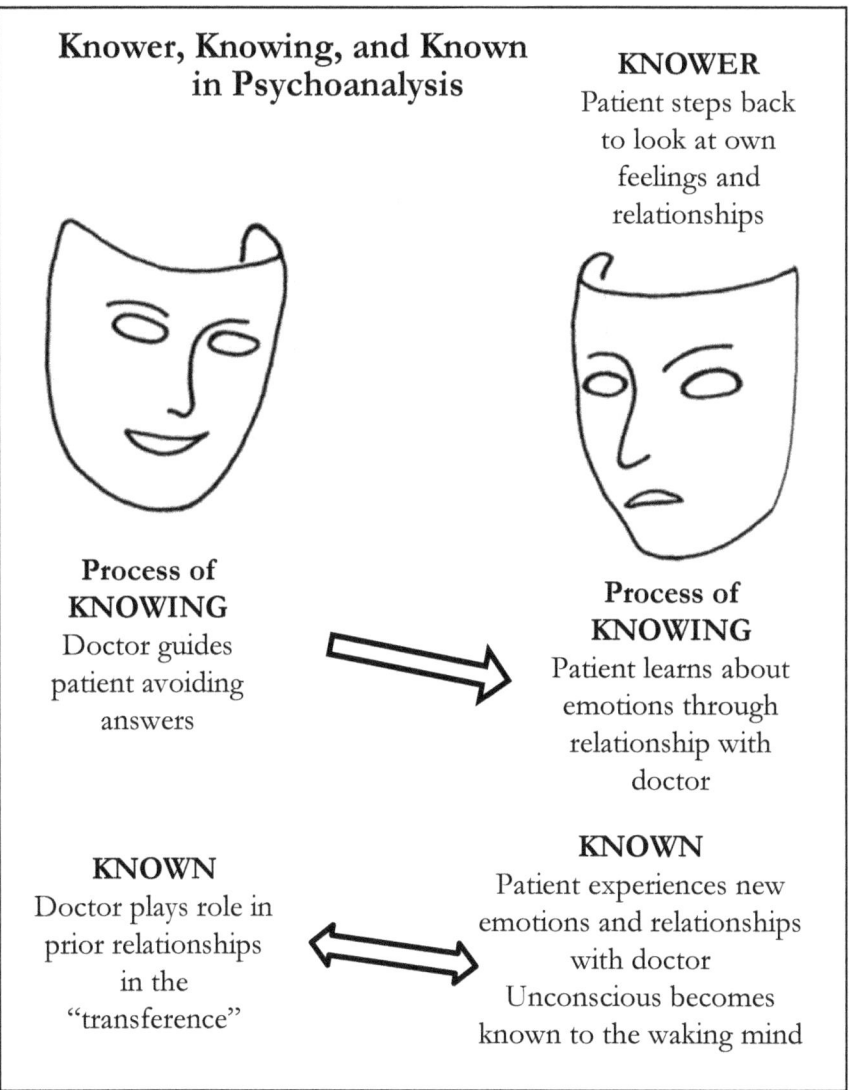

Knower, Knowing, and Known in Psychoanalysis

KNOWER
Patient steps back to look at own feelings and relationships

Process of KNOWING
Doctor guides patient avoiding answers

Process of KNOWING
Patient learns about emotions through relationship with doctor

KNOWN
Doctor plays role in prior relationships in the "transference"

KNOWN
Patient experiences new emotions and relationships with doctor
Unconscious becomes known to the waking mind

Psychoanalytic Therapies

In Psychoanalysis the patient transcends the surface of the mind but this is not so much a stepping back as a jumping in. This makes Analysis much more of a journey than CT or other talking therapies. It is an interesting journey as the destination is not known at the start. Hopefully becoming less depressed will be part of the outcome but the real destination is a more integrated mind and self-knowledge. To start with, the Known may be those unconscious ideas and feelings that need sorting out. However the final stopping place may be not just better integration but realisation of deeper parts of the psyche.

Evidence for Psychoanalysis in Depression

Analysis is such an individual therapy that the sort of evidence which modern science expects – average improvements in a large number of people compared to no therapy or another therapy – is generally lacking. Another problem is that a diagnosis of depression is not seen as useful in analytic therapies and the underlying causes or complexes are hard to categorise. Nor are the obvious symptoms of depression seen as a focus of therapy. Indeed a successful analytic journey could well involve some initial increase in depressed symptoms as you unearth and tolerate some of your problems. The length of therapy is also not a standard time and can be very long.

These difficulties in measuring and comparing the effects of analytic therapies are the major reason why Analysis has lost ground against drugs and Cognitive Therapy which are so well evidenced. Analysis can still claim to be more effective in changing our deeper personality and just as this cannot easily be proved it is not so easy to disprove it either.

Some of the briefer therapies such as Transference Focused Therapy have evidence which is growing but still relatively weak. The evidence therefore is thin in contrast to the theory which is impressive. Psychoanalytic ideas have been so persuasive that they have been a major influence on the arts and indeed on society in the last century.

It is important to emphasise that the majority of counselling available is only remotely linked to Psychoanalysis. Much counselling has some more modern and positive roots but does not have good research support. Most people like going to counselling but this does not necessarily translate into recovering from life's stresses more quickly.

Which people are comfortable with Psychoanalysis?

Psychoanalysis is not for the faint-hearted. It demands a good deal of work and tolerance of emotions. It requires open-mindedness and willingness to change. Freud observed that if anything is not up for discussion and potential change, then therapy will fail as the problems will hide in the forbidden zone. Even in our modern free-thinking era many people do have parts of their life they consider non-negotiable such as their religion or sexuality. Going into therapy with all your beliefs and values on the table for analysis is not easy.

A willingness to take responsibility is also needed. Although it may be clear that other people, like abusive parents, are historical causes, Analysis puts you in the driver's seat and challenges you to change how you are now, to create a better future. You must become the Knower and Analysis is not for someone looking for an expert to provide all the answers.

Time is an important issue to agree on before therapy starts. If you are expecting a quick fix you will be unhappy to hear after six weeks that the therapist now knows you will need a year in weekly therapy. In CT you would be preparing to say good-bye at six weeks. There are some shorter forms of analytic therapy but these require specific training for the therapist and are not widespread.

Analysis is quite an intellectual theory but the essential ingredient is being prepared to look inside your-self. If you are very set in seeing other people and their faults as being the problem you will find Analysis hard. But if you are prepared to change then using your own skills to look at your-self could be very rewarding. This is strengthening the Knower position in your mind with the Known being parts of the mind that were unconscious, leading to an expanded sense of the self.

Some emotions are so painful that they are hard to bear. These include prolonged abuse or torture – experiences anyone would rather forget. In this case if Analysis is still chosen it may be best to have learned some CBT skills first to help you tolerate distress. It is also good to have some on-going social supports otherwise it will seem a long time between sessions. Similarly, if you have a hard time tolerating emotions in general then analytic therapy will be tough. One of the leading analysts, Kernberg, suggests that the typical personality structure has changed since Freud's time and this includes a shift to more primitive defences against negative feelings. Perhaps this is another reason why Analysis has slipped down the rankings of best therapies.

How does biological depression fit in? This can be hard to disentangle because your parents provide both your genes and your family environment. If you have a strong family history of depression and strong biological symptoms these suggest there may be a chemical predisposition. But you could also have emotions and relationships that need sorting out. It is not impossible to have drugs and process therapy at the same time but it might make better sense to see how much you get out of the medication first as being the quicker option, otherwise you will not know why you are getting better. It is better not to mix analytic therapy with another type of talking therapy like Cognitive Therapy but as noted there may be a place for learning some skills before you start.

Summary

Psychoanalysis has been very influential but in its original form cannot be widely used and is poorly evidenced. There are many psychotherapies which evolved from Psychoanalysis dealing with different models of the mind, the unconscious, and our relationships. Analysis promotes self-knowledge by discovering and integrating unconscious parts of the mind. It is the most mysterious of therapies because the unconscious is such a foreign country. Psychoanalysis requires you to transcend beneath your superficial feelings and relationships. It is a more complex and demanding route than CT and the therapist is a much closer traveling companion and guide. Because there are so many schools of therapy it is vital to find a therapist with good qualifications and references.

Principles for a healthy mind identified in Analysis

∞ Parts of the mind which were unconscious can be bought to conscious awareness and integrated

∞ The patterns inside our mind parallel the patterns in our external relationships

∞ Analysing our mind can lead to more self-knowledge and expanded experience

∞ Just as we live in an external social world, our inner world has a collective level: the collective consciousness

Challenge for Psychoanalysis

The most current issues for Psychoanalysis are to find out if shorter more affordable versions work, and to provide good evidence.

Another challenge is for Psychoanalysis itself to evolve. Freud was concerned that his patients were blocked from making more progress by their defences. Psychoanalysis has had the same problem and needs to grow past its pre-occupation with the negative side of life and make more use of the positive potential in the mind. It must also look past the contents of consciousness to the field of consciousness itself.

∞ Chapter 5 ∞
Strength in Numbers
Group Therapy

Groups support our happiness through connectedness and shared activity. We have a marvellous ability to form groups almost for their own sake as being in touch with others is so important. We like to be part of something greater than our individual self and our roles in groups give us a sense of meaning in life. I am a father, a husband, a doctor and none of these roles exist without other people. Loss of role though divorce, death of a spouse, or unemployment is a powerful cause of depression as we lose connectedness, shared activities, and meaning.

Groups encompass the most central ingredients of our lives: family, work, church, politics, and our leisure pursuits. Some groups defy logic or understanding. One taxi driver in Sydney was pleased to tell me that he, like most of his village in the remote hills of Myanmar, was a supporter of Liverpool Football Club which they followed thanks to the marvel of satellite TV. The Liverpool manager once observed that "Football is not a matter of life or death – it's much more important than that." The importance lies in the connectedness of the fans.

Few people are happy to be alone and loneliness is a big factor in depression. Unfortunately this becomes a vicious circle as when you are down you may start withdrawing from friends and if you do meet up you are not the best of company. A vital task for friends when you are feeling low is for them to ensure you do not slide down this slippery slope of increasing isolation.

In the modern age we have the glory of social media which has expanded contact and communication exponentially and our chances of connection are much greater though we are still coming to terms with this opportunity. The benefits are largely obvious but there are also risks. Relationships may be more superficial, certainly less private and the warmth of a physical embrace is missing. Social media can magnify emotions whether the nasty influence of bullying or the playful enjoyment of a catchy video clip.

Group cultures

Groups have their own structures and dynamics with roles to be played and rules to be followed. Groups have goals and they have histories. In some societies groups like the family and the church are clear and stable so you know what is expected of you. This is good when things are going well for you, less good if you are being oppressed or abused in this structure. Our culture teaches us some very basic points which we may so take for granted we do not question if they might change. These include what is the expected level of mood. How happy should we expect to be? Are guilt and shame common and inevitable parts of the human condition? How do we have fun and how much fun can we have? There are also special exceptions such as festivals when we can have more fun than usual as the normal rules and restrictions are relaxed.

In collectivist cultures the group dominates over the individual. This is not just a matter of priorities or values. The nature of individual consciousness is different so that it is much harder for one person to act or live apart from the group. In this type of society there is less value placed on the happiness of an individual, more on the well-being of the larger tribe.

It is very comforting to have a strong family which will never desert you but if you are being treated badly the discomfort can be intense and long-lasting as you have nowhere to go. This has been the painful position of many abused women who find leaving too hard. Such embedded abuse affects women more than men firstly because they have less individual power in many collectivist societies and secondly because women tend to be more involved in creating social cohesion in a family or village which has positive value for the whole group. Women may help stabilise the group dynamics by accepting compromises in their own lives and therefore tolerating some level of depression.

A related situation is seen on a smaller scale in two people where one partner suffers the mood swings of Bipolar Disorder. If given a choice the other partner usually prefers the sufferer to be on the depressed side rather than in the elevated manic phase. High moods are fun but are very disruptive when you lose sensitivity to the needs of your nearest and dearest.

Group therapies

Group therapy has three major variants. Firstly there are groups in which all the participants have depression (or whatever condition is being treated) and they help each other with no therapist, often called self-help groups. In the second type there are one or sometimes two therapists leading the group. In the third type the group being treated is the natural group that includes the individual identified as being depressed which is commonly the family.

Within each variant there are many possibilities according to which therapeutic model is being used. Cognitive Behavioral Therapy is often offered in groups as it is largely didactic and one can learn from one's class mates. Self-help groups can use ideas from behavioral and cognitive models as these are accessible from books or the internet. They would be less likely to use the more complex ideas of psychoanalysis. One advantage of having a trained therapist in the group is that they bring specialised knowledge and skills. By the same token they also bring some restrictions as they stick to what they know. A self-help group could have the luxury of discussing depressive patterns of thinking using CBT one week, aromas the next and then talk about the benefit of having pets.

Therapy groups bring general benefits to a depressed person. Being depressed is normalised by meeting others also suffering. Everyone is trying to get better and hopefully they will be trying to help their fellows leading to an increase in morale. A sense of shared purpose and companionship reduces loneliness and despair. Being part of something larger than your-self is also uplifting. If a group accepts you as you are and gives you hope to change for the better, it will be a powerful support.

Group therapies use knowledge from the individual therapy schools but there are other special ingredients that come from the group dynamics. These are particularly strong in family therapy where the group is already a powerful unit. In a group comprised of people previously strangers the group culture is strengthened by setting rules. Meeting regularly and on time and maintaining confidentiality are some basic conditions. There are clearly agreed rules of behavior within the group or outside it. Self-help groups may deliberately blur the boundary with social support outside the group sessions and they can become the basis of long-term social relationships. A psychoanalytic group on the other hand is more likely to discourage outside contacts so that the sessions themselves become a more distinct part of life. Strong group boundaries make for a strong group dynamic and strong collective consciousness.

At an extreme there are Encounter groups where very strong boundaries are set up around the group such as going to a different location for longer sessions. Then the normal barriers between individuals inside the group are broken down sometimes leading to very physical encounters which have their obvious risks.

Family groups have their own structure and dynamics. These can be used therapeutically as well as being seen as causes of depression. A man is alcoholic and the only way his wife can stabilise the family is to be depressed. The individual depressed client is not the problem here. We need to deal with the couple at least. Why is the husband drinking so much? There may be further complexities. Is he working too hard in order to support the family? Does he prefer being away from home because he cannot deal with his wife when she is depressed? Are they both avoiding dealing with teenage children?

Families have several special forms of communication due to their very close and long-term relationships. The "double bind" is when two choices are presented neither of which are right. Your mother tells you that leaving home means you do not love her but staying at home means she has not brought you up to be strong and independent. Depression can result as any positive move is judged to be bad.

Depression in one person may be a reaction to unpleasant things happening in the family but it can also have a positive role. A depressed child may be bringing his parents together in their common desire to help her. One of the strongest dynamics is that of homeostasis. Just as the body has mechanisms to keep blood pressure, glucose levels etc. steady, families have mechanisms to keep relationships in balance. When someone is persistently depressed we might wonder if the current balance is not working for them. This is an opportunity for promoting a crisis which allows for the balance to be reset. In systemic family therapies crises are very much seen as positive opportunities which is a very different approach to focussing on reducing the symptoms of depression in one individual. It might help for them to become more depressed in the short term so the system they are living in is forced to change.

Paradoxical success

Madeleine had a dreadful childhood being abused by one parent and neglected by the other. She was naturally bright and went as far as starting college but dropped out because of her persistent depression and acts of self-harm. She cut herself because she felt she deserved to suffer and as a way of controlling her severe distress.

She tried medications and possibly had some response to an antidepressant but this was hard to say as she did not persist or she took over-doses. Psychological therapy did not go well as she could not trust her therapists to take care of her. DBT might have been a good choice as she had Borderline traits but there was no local group available.

What did work for her was joining a group. This was not a therapy group but more of an interest or study group looking at anti-psychiatry. At first glance this seemed a poor choice for someone who looked to need more and better therapy not less. However the group was great for her. Madeleine had a strong dislike of being dependent as she did not trust others but at the same time she felt helpless and forced to lean on other people for emotional strength. She was fortunate to find through this group a close friendship with a man who did not buy into the illness and treatment model which had not worked for her so far. His personal philosophy, backed up by the group, enabled him to provide enough care and attention but at the same time push her to recognise her strengths and the necessity of being more independent. This is a rare skill especially when the recipient of such attention presents such a high risk of suicide. Most of us bale out into taking too much control.

She survived this paradoxical therapy which was not a therapy and her self-esteem improved. She continued to struggle with depression for some time but the frequent suicidal thoughts were replaced by an increasing hope that life could be different. The group introduced her to a new way of seeing herself and also to an important individual friendship.

Roles and skills

Marriage and family roles are complex and hard to learn if we have not picked them up from our early role models. Specific skills are much easier to learn. A significant development in the last generation has been the increased recognition that people with mental illness are skills deficient and that learning these skills is very helpful. Some are included in the CBT approach, especially problem solving, while others may be taught in wider and less clinical settings, such as communication, assertiveness and conflict resolution strategies. Some people lack very basic abilities of recognising and modulating their own emotions. Teaching these is a central part of DBT.

Skills' training has a simple didactic approach with a set curriculum, teaching, practice and usually homework. It is just like school and indeed some school programs round the world are teaching these skills.

One particular skill that can be taught is meditation. We may not think of this as a normal ability but it is like language, a natural ability which nevertheless needs learning. Being able to settle your mind down has many advantages in depression as we see in a later chapter and it is a central element in the mind fully maturing

Group consciousness

Every group has a collective mind, a collective consciousness. Just as an individual has a personality, we can also characterise a family, a city, a nation or a therapy group. The stronger the group identity the more powerful this level is and the more work it can do in therapy. Especially in the analytic therapies the group itself becomes the main ingredient. Strong boundaries allow more freedom and safety within the group sessions which allows more expression and understanding of our emotions and relationships.

Freud showed how our personal mental dynamics are reflected in our external relationships and the same will happen in the group. We project our inner world out onto the group. We treat other participants as people in our past and present lives. This tendency is used overtly in some therapies such as Psycho-drama where we are encouraged to enact the inner dramas of our less conscious mind with the group members playing different roles for us.

Jung saw the large scale collective consciousness as being mostly unconscious, powerful but hidden and revealing itself through dreams and myths. In groups we experience a smaller and more obvious group consciousness. The team spirit in a football game or the joyful atmosphere of a dance hall is very easily felt. In group therapy where the boundaries are strong we can create a focussed and intense collective consciousness. This collective mind may speak through individual members, when one person speaks but their feelings are reflective of the whole group. One reason for having a skilled therapist is for them to be able to recognise and work with the group level feelings and dynamics. If a positive group consciousness is developed this accelerates the progress of all the individual members.

Social contagion

Increased connectedness should mean less depression if it is true that social integration is so healthy. However it does depend on who your friends are, and not just your immediate friends but even the friends of friends of your friends. There is increasing evidence that low mood is contagious not through some physical virus but through our social networks. Friends and peers seem to be more influential than family in this effect. The mechanism is not proven but presumably we copy other people and try to fit in with their way of thinking. Some individuals are higher status in the network and if they promote negative attitudes or push depressing material down the net-work we can be dragged down. "Co-rumination" is a nice new term for getting caught up in some-one else's negativity.

How do we counter this danger? The most obvious way is to be a positive influence ourselves and remember that sharing sorrow does not always reduce it. Spending time with people who lift your mood is another basic strategy. This should not mean abandoning friends who are going through a hard time but when supporting someone who is depressed you are not obliged to co-ruminate and this is not helpful to them. Having a wider network is also useful so you are less prone to being overwhelmed by a small number of people in a low state. Another defence is to have good emotional resilience yourself and so be less vulnerable to other people's stress.

Cooperation and evolution

Cooperation is crucial to humanity's success and has given us an evolutionary advantage. The sophistication of a modern society demands that we specialise in our roles and cooperate to create our complex civilisation. Integrating the demands and needs of individuals and the group is challenging but rewarding. The music of an orchestra is much richer than the sum of its individual players.

Playing with others is a skill we learn as young children though some learn this better than others. In adult life the ability and tendency to cooperate is very variable and is one measure of maturity. Whether in the family, at work, or at play the ability to see the needs of others and of the whole group is extremely valuable. For a village or small tribe in a more primitive setting cooperation is patently necessary to allow survival of the group. Families do not have the luxury of tolerating many individuals who are non-productive when the whole group is barely managing to get enough to eat. In a wealthy urban society we do have this luxury but it is easily abused.

In the modern family tribal links are lower in value than our immediate family bonds and the relationship of mother to child is the source of much psychoanalytic theory. The romantic partnership between two adults is the inspiration for most of our modern music. Unfortunately we do seem to be stuck at the early romantic and sexual side of this and have much less confidence around the more permanent marriage relationship. A good marriage can provide companionship, practical and financial support, children, social stability and love. It is so important that this bond is held as sacred in most cultures. A happy marriage certainly provides a strong resistance to depression.

The prevalence of depression parallels our social instability including the weakness and transience of our marriages. Clearly there are many possible social structures and while serial monogamy may be good for some, for many multiple marriages are not a series of successes but a repetition of failure.

Marital therapy does its best but there is not great evidence that it works. Modern culture is very focussed on loving oneself, on individual life, individual happiness and rights. We are weak on altruism, responsibility and love for others. Tinkering around with the surface values of behavior and thinking patterns may be useful to defuse conflict but will not achieve mutual love. For this we need a higher level of maturity to form a truly trusting respectful and intimate relationship. To become as one with another person and yet retain ones individuality is a microcosm of our spiritual potential to become one with God or cosmic intelligence while remaining an individual.

Suicide

At the other end of evolutionary choices is suicide, a statement that an individual's life is so bad it has to end. Self-harm and suicide are not pleasant topics and many countries have media restrictions on the reporting of suicide. This is to reduce copy-cat deaths especially in youth but it also reflects our avoidance of discussing what has become a major embarrassing problem. In developed countries there are about as many deaths from suicide as from traffic accidents and suicide is a leading cause of death in young adults. What does this tell us about our culture?

If we medicalise suicide we shall say that depression is the major cause and certainly depression does play a part. However the types of depression present are often those where personality weaknesses or loneliness are present. Borderline personality style with its difficulty managing distress, lability of mood, and impulsiveness is present in up to a third of suicides. Loneliness and lack of connection to others is a frequent finding. This applies to individuals but also to whole groups who are disempowered or alienated such as indigenous people in developed countries.

Unfortunately alcohol is now a dominant part of social relationships for many. Alcohol can reduce anxiety and ease social contact but it also has the power to depress mood and reduce inhibitions making impulsive self harm easier. Alcohol is a common facilitator in completed suicide.

Religion used to be more of a barrier to suicide as it was a central connection for society and gave meaning and hope to our lives. With the medicalisation of death there is less questioning of what happens after death. Curiously many people contemplating suicide have not asked themselves this question or just assume there is nothing.

Every suicide is a tragedy and those left behind ask themselves what could we have done and should we have seen this would happen. We do have very good predictors of overall suicide risk looking at drug and alcohol use, mental illness, personality, social stress etc. However we are not at all good at predicting exactly when someone will attempt suicide. This is no different to heart disease where the population factors of blood pressure, smoking etc. are well known but each cardiac event is still a sudden shock. As in heart disease some of the risk factors are widespread in the population. In fact if you ask adults if they have had suicidal thoughts in the last year a staggering 7% have and half the population have seriously considered suicide at some point in their life.

To address the high level of suicides we do need to have better access to treatment but more importantly we need to create a society where people have more meaning in their life, more supports and one where life itself is recognised as having an infinite value. There are some excellent public health campaigns to reduce the stigma of depression and improve the chance of people seeking help. These also promote caring and support from family and friends. Other initiatives include teaching resiliency, communication and problem-solving skills in school. These are all great but we also require a stronger spiritual life and how to achieve this is less easy to agree on.

Richard in Group Therapy

In this incarnation Richard is recommended to a group by his GP. There is a well-established men's group running locally and it happens in the evening allowing people to come after work. It is also less expensive than private one-to-one therapy. Richard is anxious about going but has enough insight to realise that others may have similar problems to him and especially other men. The group does cover themes of achieving work goals under stress, forming a loving relationship and indeed drinking. There is a group leader who works more as a facilitator than a therapist and the members of the group are encouraged to come up with their own suggestions and solutions.

Richard quite enjoys being one of the class rather than the teacher but he also finds himself often offering ideas and support as he is used to speaking to a group. He is surprised how much his views are listened to and starts to wonder why he never took his own advice in the past.

Simple ideas like limiting drinking to reduce negative effects do seem more real when agreed on by others with similar experiences. Similarly it seems obvious to treat your girl-friend with more respect and find out what she really wants. In a way the group allows Richard to reflect on his situation with more openness and honesty as fellow participants act as good lie detectors.

The group is not into complex or deep psychological analysis but many of the simple ideas from Behavioral and Cognitive approaches come out albeit in an indirect way. There is also more recognition of people's values and roles. What is of most importance to Richard and which parts of his life need the most attention? Although his teaching role is important to him and seems to be under stress, it is his relationship and leisure time which are really stuck and putting stress back on his work life. Drinking is a compounding factor.

Richard was not looking for life-long mates and does not keep up with his group members afterwards but he did greatly value their time together. The group effect was strong and he retained clear memories of the work they did together.

Knower, Knowing and Known

One of the joys of group therapy is that we can play more complicated therapy games and take different roles. You can be the observer of others to learn from them, or present your own problems and solutions to be known by them. You can be the facilitator enhancing the group's ability to learn more. Role playing of situations is a part of many groups. This allows a more immediate experience than just talking about a relationship or interaction and helps us to practice and learn new skills.

Self-help groups are particularly flexible due to their lack of hierarchy and you may like them for this reason. There is no expert or director and no chance of becoming dependent on the therapist. We all bring our own history, knowledge, and roles. If you are used to being the one who is dependent or listens passively in the family then this may be pointed out to you in the group and you can choose to try out some different scripts.

Depressed people commonly become withdrawn and less assertive. If this is part of your personality style then learning to be more active in the group discussions and relationships can itself be useful. On the other hand if you tend to talk too much and not listen to others, then recognising that other people do have good advice for you may be beneficial.

The therapists too have more potential roles in a group. In a teaching style of therapy the therapist is mainly in the Knower role. In analytic therapy, as for individual work, he takes the Knowing position encouraging the group members to become the Knowers. A popular set-up is for one therapist to relate to individual members and a second therapist to watch for and respond to the group consciousness. Many other relationships are possible. Two therapists could interact with each other to demonstrate how to resolve arguments. One therapist could defend a patient's position while another challenges it to stimulate discussion.

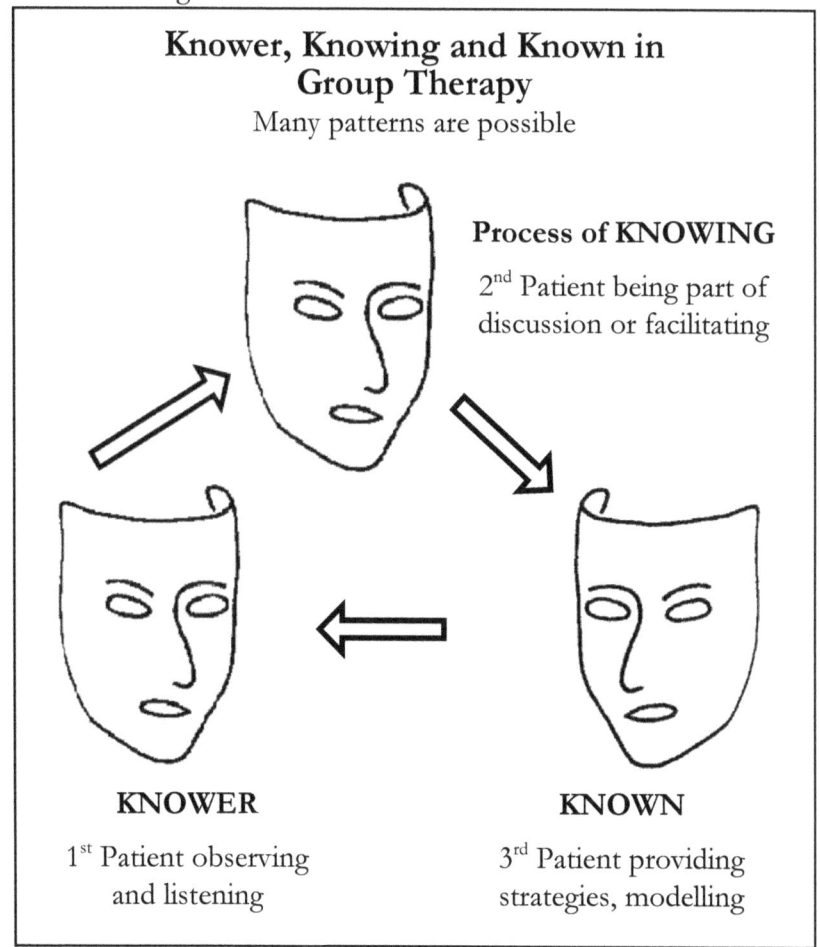

Knower, Knowing and Known in Group Therapy
Many patterns are possible

Process of KNOWING
2nd Patient being part of discussion or facilitating

KNOWER
1st Patient observing and listening

KNOWN
3rd Patient providing strategies, modelling

In family therapy the group will naturally continue to function in normal life when the therapy is over. Therefore it is very important that they do not become dependent on the therapist. Family

Group Therapy

therapists are careful not to become the only Knower and they often keep therapy short.

Effectiveness of Group Therapy in Depression

How effective groups are depends on the type of depression you have, the appropriateness of the group, and the quality of the therapist. CBT groups are well evidenced and it should be easy enough to check your therapist is qualified. Some specific support groups such as those for Bipolar illness are also well established and have become part of the accepted best practice for treatment. For the depression associated with Borderline Personality Disorder, Dialectic Behavioral Therapy (DBT), which uses both individual and group therapy, is now well evidenced but it is vital you have properly credentialed therapists.

Skills' training is well established as effective in teaching particular skills. It is harder to judge if a specific skill is critical in your depression. Most likely it will be one ingredient. Becoming more assertive or a better problem solver may not immediately change your life but it can lead to longer term changes and there is evidence that even brief problem solving training reduces future acts of self-harm.

Family therapy is widely available but there are a bewildering number of approaches. As the presenting problem, such as one person being depressed, may not be the fundamental issue and because it is hard to measure how a family improves, it is more difficult to establish numerical proof of effectiveness. Again, having an experienced therapist is vital and therapy should usually be brief.

Analytical groups have the same problem with establishing proof. By its nature this approach usually takes longer so you need to stay with the program to get results. It will be more useful where there are complex emotional factors in your depression such as prior abuse which are not so amenable to a bit of cognitive restructuring.

Self-help groups vary greatly and here the success of the group depends on the commitment and capacity of the members. You need to enter with the intention to contribute as well as receive. This is true for all groups but with no therapist to remind you it is more obvious here.

Whatever type of group you go for you should have some idea of what you want to achieve. This can be clearly spelled out in CBT and DBT and it is simple if you go to a group teaching a specific skill like assertiveness. For family therapy you should have a more open agenda as just improving the mood or changing the behavior of one person is not likely to be enough. Similarly in analytic groups you are seeking deeper improvement than just being less depressed. In self-help, are you looking for a short membership to help you though a low period or are you after a longer term support group?

Which people are comfortable with Group Therapy?

Groups may be too threatening for extremely shy people. If the group is well focussed and has a clear curriculum, as in a CBT group, the social demands are much less and you may benefit from the limited social interaction.

For less structured groups you need to be able to accept feedback. A paranoid attitude would be less than ideal. Groups best suit people who are flexible in their Knower, Knowing and Known positions. You should be able to listen as well as talk.

Financially, group therapy is cheaper. It does require commitment to attending and session times will not be flexible. As with any group activity it works better if everyone turns up. Some groups have very tight rules to strengthen the collective consciousness which might include not being able to enter once the group has started or having to leave if you miss more than one session. Do check beforehand if you cannot commit to the rules. Group therapy seems a less intense option than individual where you are in focus all the time. For CBT and skills training this might be true but other groups do have their own intensity and are not a softer option.

Groups are great if you are feeling all alone in your problem and would like others' support. You may also want to try joining normal non-therapeutic groups. If you are taking medication or going for individual therapy there will be no harm in also increasing your social and recreational contact with others. In the long term this is a good path towards staving off future depressions.

Summary

Connectedness through groups is part of a healthy happy life and there are many useful group therapies. Their growth shows our human tendency to do things together including learning. Groups help counteract our restrictive focus on the individual and give us an experience of a positive group consciousness. They are pragmatically a good use of the limited number of skilled therapists available.

Any type of therapy can be done in a group setting from the teaching style of CBT to the more open style of analytic therapies. Where the individual depression is seen to be a manifestation of a natural group like the family then group therapy is essential.

Principles for a healthy mind identified in Group Therapy

∞ Individual happiness is supported by positive groups
∞ The collective mind is more than the sum of the individuals
∞ Strong collective consciousness supports healing in the individual mind

Challenge for Group therapy

We live in an exciting time when social connectedness is rising through electronic means but we are challenged by the weakness of traditional groups such as religion and family. Having established the individual as primary we are now busy reconnecting en masse. The underlying field of consciousness that connects us at depth is experienced in a local way in a therapy group reminding us that we are not alone. Society's challenge is to use the new electronic connectedness to promote mental well-being. One part of this is making therapy available over the Internet. More important will be whether happiness or depression becomes more contagious in social media.

Electronic gadgets are evolving fast. The parallel challenge is for us to use the technology of our own brains and consciousness to network not through screens but directly in the medium of collective group consciousness.

∞ Chapter 6 ∞
Magic Bullets
Biological Psychiatry

A healthy mind needs a healthy body. We all know this but what exactly does a healthy body mean and how do we achieve it? Do we go to the gym and tone up our muscles or is it better to take drugs and balance our brain chemistry? An astounding one in ten of adult Americans does take an anti-depressant according to the latest National Health and Nutrition Examination Survey. This increases to one in four for middle aged women. Is it OK that Prozac is such a household name?

Depression does have a strong genetic factor which means some of us are more prone than others but we do not fully understand how this risk is carried in the physiology. The drug company money is on the neuro-transmitter systems with which the anti-depressant drugs interact but this is not the only area of the body worth looking at. We can also usefully consider our level of activity, biological rhythms and physical illness.

It would be simpler if anti-depressant drugs only worked for people with a biologically driven depression but life is not so easy. Depression is confusing because we commonly find both genetic predisposition and situational factors. Often there are obvious reasons for depression in terms of difficult life circumstances and events. If you live in poverty, without social support and important people have died, you are more likely to be depressed. Luckily, but perhaps curiously, anti-depressants may still be of some help even if there are clear psychological causes for your depression. They do not just work for endogenous depression caused by internal genetically driven mood imbalances. Many clinicians would see a sufferer as having a genetic tendency or vulnerability to depression which is then precipitated by loss and adverse circumstances. Within the biological sphere are additional stresses of life-style, alcohol abuse or physical illness.

Jim was a smart man and knew he had unresolved emotions regarding his family but they were simply too painful and he did not want to dig them up. He had not done cognitive therapy as such but had learned some related skills in management training and this did not appeal as a route. Taking a simple view, his current life was good at work and at home and he was nevertheless depressed so he was keen to try medication.

His family doctor prescribed a standard anti-depressant and he did indeed feel much better in a few weeks. One problem arose, a failing to rise to the occasion sexually. This was an unacceptable side effect and was not improved on the second drug tried. The third, from a less used group, the MAOI's, maintained his mood improvement without this side-effect so all was well.

Jim was 60 years old and had been a successful manager who struggled with depression several times in his life. His wife died of cancer which bought back very painful memories of his mother's death when he was a teenager and the family was in turmoil. He coped by focusing on his work which he was good at and on exercise. He recovered enough to start a new relationship and re-married to a bright and active lady. His social life and exercise, through dancing, increased but a few months later he again became more depressed, was barely able to stay at work and sought medical help.

He had a strong family history for depression and his mother had in fact committed suicide almost certainly when depressed. This points to a genetic risk for Jim and indicates medication may be useful. However there were equally strong psychological factors. Clearly having your mother commit suicide when you are growing up is a terrible trauma. This was compounded by his father becoming alcoholic and the family fragmenting as people blamed each other for the suicide. This would all indicate a place for psycho-therapy. Jim had had some life-style issues but had dealt very positively to these with exercise, diet, and moderation in alcohol. He had a tendency to overwork as an escape but did not go too far and his re-marriage addressed this balance well.

Jim was then left with the tricky question of how long to remain on the medication and he agreed with his doctor to go for a standard 6 months though some would have advised longer given his prior episodes. When he came off he again felt down though not as bad as before. His life and life-style were now going very well so he applied the previously logic and returned to the medication planning to stay on another year.

Different experts would have their own explanations for Jim. A psychoanalyst would naturally point out that his unresolved emotions were still there even if unconscious. A spiritual perspective might be useful given his mother's death and Jim's own increasing age. An alternative health practitioner might want to look in more detail at his diet and habits. The pharmacological approach is simply that he has a genetic depressive tendency and needs to stay on the drugs. Jim agreed with this approach even though he did not dismiss the possible truth of other explanations.

Perhaps as a society we have made this same choice and tolerated 10% of the adult population being on antidepressants. For people on an anti-depressant less than a third of them have seen a mental health professional in the last year and one in seven of people on these drugs have been taking them for over 10 years. For many of us the other ways of looking at depression are not being considered.

We could say Jim's treatment is a good result for drug therapy but is it a good reflection on society that so many of us need to be on medication for so long?

Burn out

We saw earlier that our level of activity is an important place to start. Too much is stressful and this can be seen at a chemical level. There is a cascade of transmitters and stress hormones going from the Hypothalamus to the Pituitary to the Adrenal gland to the rest of the body (HPA axis). This ramps up when we are stressed to allow us to have more energy and drive. If it is running hot for too long it burns up and we feel it. We are exhausted and unable to lift ourselves, burnt out or running on empty with the system no longer responding to demands for more. Too much activity can mean too much physical activity but often it is mental overdrive and our physical exercise may actually be low.

Stress is a good candidate for Agent Blue, the cause of depression increasing in modern times. There are many types of stress including poverty, politics, and relationships. One aspect of modern stress is that our response, which comes from a previous time in evolution, is not appropriate. You spend the day in the office on the computer or in meetings. When stressed your body's response is good for running and fighting – tempting but not generally good strategies in the office. We have less overall exercise than in previous eras and less physical outlets for stress. Regular exercise is good for stress and has been clearly shown to be useful in depression.

If your total level of movement is very low this predisposes you to obesity and metabolic problems and also to depression. How much time do you spend sitting down? A happy medium is needed for physical exercise and this is best built into the daily routine because once you have become depressed starting up new exercise regimes is hard indeed.

Biological rhythms

The normal rhythm of waking and sleeping turns out to be critical in depression. One of the strongest markers for future depression is an abnormal sleep rhythm. Typically in depression the dream sleep or Rapid Eye Movement (REM) sleep pattern is abnormal. REM sleep occurs normally every 90 minutes, the first time being 90 minutes after falling asleep. In depression REM sleep starts earlier and gets used up earlier followed by early morning waking. People prone to depression show some abnormality in this direction even between episodes. Some scientists consider depression to be primarily an abnormality of circadian rhythm. This pattern is likely present if you notice that you get off to sleep OK but wake up very early and cannot then get back to sleep.

Jet lag and shift work are situations in which we are forced to move our day-night rhythm and this may well alter our mood giving us at least a brief taste of depression. While it used to be thought that sufferers from depression just had poor sleep secondary to their depression it is also true that poor sleep patterns can change your mood. The best practice for Bipolar Disorder now includes attention to a good daily routine and sleep pattern. Enough sleep and regularity of the timing of sleep are important and healthy. Jet lag occurs when we cross time zones and stress our internal clocks. If you have a history of mood disorder there is some increased risk of episodes being precipitated. Westward travel tends to trigger depression while eastward may start off a manic swing but the effect is variable. General advice to mitigate the time stress is to be well rested before traveling, not drinking alcohol, keeping well hydrated, and taking exercise at the destination.

There is no simple way to restore a good sleep pattern other than developing good habits and avoiding things that stress the clocks like caffeine and alcohol. Anti-depressant drugs may help with sleep either as a sedative side-effect or as a consequence of the depression improving. Disappointingly they do not restore a normal sleep pattern and tend to greatly reduce, even abolish, REM sleep. This explains why intense rebound dreaming can occur after stopping these medicines.

One of the least used strategies for depression is the paradoxical sleep deprivation therapy. You stay up one entire night and the next day, i.e. stay up and awake for 36 hours. With luck your sleep routine then snaps back into a more normal pattern. If a depression seems strongly biological and you cannot take anti-depressants this might be considered.

One of the explanations for why women are more at risk of depression is that their circadian rhythm is more easily disturbed. The additional monthly hormonal changes make the daily clock more vulnerable probably due to varying oestrogen levels. Ladies are also more likely to suffer Seasonal Affective Disorder (SAD) which causes depression in the winter. This happens more towards the North Pole as not many people live near the South Pole. SAD is atypical in that sleep and appetite increase and can be seen as a mild form of hibernation. Fortunately Light Therapy is very effective and starts working very quickly. This can be achieved by running brighter full spectrum lights in your home or, if time and money allow, by skiing holidays which also gives you some exercise and social group therapy.

Women have times of vulnerability directly related to their reproductive system. Pre-menstrual mood disorder is commonly found with the other rhythm disorders of insomnia and SAD. It may respond to anti-depressants but it is definitely worth trying to get your routines in best order first. The hormonal and psychological changes around the time of delivering a child are immense and there is a strong risk then of depression, especially if you have any other risk factors like a Bipolar tendency. The changes at the time of menopause are more gradual but they are large in extent making this another vulnerable time. There is some advocacy for hormonal treatment rather than anti-depressants but this is not accepted by all.

Richard and the Biological Psychiatrist

Most drug therapy is prescribed not by psychiatrists but by primary care or family doctors. Richard is not seen as ill enough to merit specialist referral and is treated in primary care. The simplest level of analysis is that he has a second episode of depression with no evidence of Bipolar illness so an anti-depressant is prescribed. Most doctors would have a wider view than just drug therapy and hopefully the time to give some of the behavioral advice to take time off, exercise, and drink less alcohol, but they may not have the time to follow up in detail. The doctor's own bias towards drug therapy would also be a factor.

The choice of drug is important. Richard's doctor advises an SSRI which is not sedating, as he still wants to work full-time. Richard has to accept that there will not be much positive effect for two weeks which feels like long time to him but he sticks it out. Fortunately he does not have any major side effects which would have meant a change of medications and another waiting period.

He does start to feel better, less worried and more able to focus on his work. He feels less pressure and his mood is better though not quite back to normal. This assistance supports him through the end of term and in the vacation he has time off and makes further recovery. Next term he copes better but has not made any great changes to his work situation and continues to feel vulnerable. He has taken some more exercise but not really drunk much less. As he has been depressed before his doctor advises him to stay on the medication for at least a year and he agrees.

During the next months he reflects more on his life-style with his girl-friend's encouragement and makes some improvements. It is almost a year before he feels back to normal and fully enjoying life. He has not yet made any changes to his supports at work. He then stops the medicines without drama except for a bit of dreaming rebound. Three months later he is depressed again and restarts the medicines, his mood brightening again but not feeling 100%.

Richard would count as a positive responder to medication as he improved significantly but he did not get back to his usual level of mood, energy and optimism. Hopefully he would not accept this as his new lower quality of life. It is unlikely he will do much better on another drug and his doctor should point him in the direction of either life-style changes or psychotherapy to add to the medication effect.

If you have had more than one episode of depression, like Richard, or become depressed later in life, studies show that statistically very long-term antidepressant treatment could be useful in reducing further episodes. What is less studied is how much protection you can get from changing your exercise level and daily routine.

Bipolar Disorder

Bipolar disorder is the most convincingly biological type of mood disorder, firstly because it has a high genetic component and secondly as it looks different to a psychological depression. Bipolar swings are often sudden and while they may be triggered by events they also happen spontaneously. The upside of Bipolar disorder is mania or hypo- (less than) mania. This is the opposite of depression and in small amounts gives not just a happy mood but also more drive, energy, less sleep, faster more creative thinking. Too high a mood renders us reckless, disinhibited and moving along to be paranoid and grandiose to a delusional degree. Left to them-selves upward mood swings typically last 2-3 months compared to downward swings of around 3-6 months but each person has their own pattern.

The fact that a small increase in mood can make us more successful may explain why the Bipolar gene is so prevalent and why we often find creative and high-powered relatives in these families. Many great politicians have only needed a few hours of sleep and have high energy levels, suggesting their base-line mood is higher than the average. A very positive self-image may be another of their strengths. For the population in general the base-line or average mood is lower than ideal, just as so many of us have too high a weight, blood pressure, or cholesterol.

Most Bipolar sufferers consider the suffering of depression worse than the up-swings though these may cause more disruption. Their partners may well prefer them to be a bit more down than up as life is quieter then. One patient of mine went through an up and a down swing and came out the other end in a stable good mood. He looked entirely well to me being appropriately assertive with his rather demanding family. They complained bitterly because he was no longer the mildly depressed submissive man he had been prior to the swings. His baseline had shifted.

Best treatment for Bipolar disorder includes taking a mood stabilising drug, keeping a stable daily routine especially sleep time, and belonging to a Bipolar support group. This last is advised because you are more likely to listen to your peers with Bipolar disorder than professionals or family. This particularly refers to the up-swings when the boundary between a good mood and a too good harmful mood is hard to judge for your-self. Other strategies include having a grasp of your early warning signs, such as reduced sleep time, to manage swings before they get out of hand.

Medication for Bipolar disorder is interesting because anti-depressants are avoided. These medicines push mood up but are likely to either trigger manic swings or to make mood less stable and flip you into more frequent swings. When Bipolar becomes rapid cycling it is much harder to treat.

The mood stabilising drugs include Lithium, which is chemically related to Sodium, several of the anti-convulsant drugs, and some of the anti-psychotic drugs. They are effective, sometimes magically so, other times less, but with average reduction of episodes by about a factor of three. Unfortunately they can have side effects and detailed attention to choice of drug, dose and timing is very worth-while. Pregnancy is not advisable on most of the drugs, added to which childbirth can trigger Bipolar episodes, so very careful discussion and planning are needed here.

A new approach to treatment is taking Omega 3 fatty acids as in fish oil and research is on-going with some optimism. People with mood disorders often have lower levels of Omega 3, which is low in the Western diet, and countries with higher fish consumption tend to have lower rates of depression. The evidence is not strong enough to change the existing therapy guidelines but it is a promising possibility.

Mood lability

Most of us do not have the up and down periods of Bipolar disorder which typically last for a few months if untreated. We do all have some variation in our mood from day to day and hour to hour. This is a clear personality trait with some people being by nature more stable in their mood whatever is happening around them and others more volatile. This volatility, or lability as we call it clinically, can be troubling. Some reactivity of mood is expected and makes you look human, interested in and responding to life, but if you over-react to minor stimuli and cannot calm yourself down easily you seem immature or hard to live with. "High maintenance" is a polite label.

Too much lability is a key characteristic of the Borderline personality and there is some dispute as whether this in turn is related to a form of Bipolar tendency. The aetiology of Borderline personality is contentious but many like Linehan's formulation that there is a constitutional tendency to labile mood plus an invalidating childhood which prevented sufferers learning how to identify and manage their feelings. Rapid mood changes drive cognitive distortions, stress relationships, and lead to damaging ways of controlling distress such as cutting one-self. Sense of self is unstable with reliance on the opinion of others even though trust of others is low, often following abuse. The good news is that this syndrome is treatable and one of the keys from Linehan's therapy, DBT, is learning skills to deal with and reduce mood lability.

While Borderline syndrome may have a biological component the main therapy is psychological. Drugs are often sought but are not very effective. It is particularly important not to let the biological approach undermine the psychological one. Looking for a better medication can distract a patient from learning and using better strategies to cope with their mood and life in general.

Physical illness

We have all experienced some symptoms of depression when we have flu or another infection. Being physically weak tends to lower our mood and this effect is stronger for long term illnesses. There are many reasons for this. Physical illness pushes different chemicals such as inflammatory response elements into the blood which directly makes us feel lethargic. Psychologically, being ill prevents us enjoying our usual work and family activities. Pain and other discomforts are directly distressing experiences which wear us down over time. We may also have fears of disability or death.

Cardiovascular disease has a special association with depression and it is no coincidence that both are so common. Even from a young age cardiovascular illness factors are a predictor for depression. Likewise depression predicts increased risk of heart and arterial disease. There are several physiological factors linking these two conditions. One is the disturbed functioning in the HPA or stress hormone system. Another is variability in the autonomic nervous system which directly affects the heart rate and rhythm. Poor diet, inactivity and smoking can play their roles. Another less well known chemical factor may be the body's inflammatory chemicals such as cytokines which can reduce serotonin.

Many other illnesses have been studied including cancer which is obviously a potentially depressing disease to have. Avoiding depression, maintaining hope, and keeping up a fight to be well can improve your outcome and quality of life.

A recent link has been made between sleep apnoea and depression and selling machines to reduce this problem has become a boom industry. For many sufferers losing weight is a more curative path and there are practical tips to avoid sleeping on your back involving ping-pong balls or baseball caps. Singing lessons can help strengthen the muscles at the back of the palate. Sleep apnoea disturbs your sleep and can reduce the level of oxygen in the blood directly affecting brain functioning.

Which bullets have the most magic?

There are a bewildering number of anti-depressants but they fall into a few categories. The first are the directly stimulant drugs which some of us might own up to having tried as illegal recreational drugs. These are brilliant drugs in that they give a large and rapid lift to your mood. The huge down side is that you tend to crash into a worse depression afterwards. Addiction is rapid with dose escalation and deterioration of the personality. There are some legally prescribed stimulants which tend to be used more in the USA than many other developed countries. Typically they would be considered when less potentially risky drugs have failed as the risk of addiction remains high. The prescribed drugs include traditional stimulants, Dexamphetamine and Methylphenidate, and newer drugs like Modafinil. They have not been shown to have a useful role in the on-going term therapy of depression and their role as adjunctive drugs, or drugs to be used while waiting for other anti-depressants to work, is not established. They tend to work better on the secondary symptoms of depression like tiredness, fatigue and lack of concentration but they do not have a well-evidenced place in therapy for depression currently.

The first major group of anti-depressant prescribed drugs was the tri-cyclics which refers to their chemical structure. The main ones are Amitriptyline and Imipramine. They are effective but have numerous side effects including dry mouth, constipation and blurred vision. The dose needed for a good response is not far from the dose giving too many side-effects so careful adjustment of doses is needed. Another problem is that they are very dangerous in overdose.

A second group which has been around for some time is the Mono-amine-oxidase Inhibitors (MAOI's). Serotonin, Norepinephrine and Dopamine are all monoamines and these drugs delay their metabolism meaning they persist for longer at the nerve endings. The earlier versions had major issues with restrictions on diet and other prescribed drugs with bad effects on the heart and blood pressure if not adhered to. The more recent drugs such as Moclobemide only affect one sub-type of MAO so have far fewer problems. However they are less used mainly due to the success of the next group.

The next development was of drugs specifically dealing with Serotonin, the Selective Serotonin Reuptake Inhibitors (SSRI's). As they hit fewer receptors they have fewer side effects but they still have some, including nausea, head-aches and sexual problems. Dosing is much easier with most people taking the standard dose and they are much safer in overdose. There has been a spirited debate as to whether some people at least temporarily become more suicidal on these drugs and their use in adolescents has been especially curtailed. Some people certainly do experience an increase in activation early on and this may be experienced as anxiety, agitation or possibly suicidal thoughts.

More recent drugs are those that hit both serotonin and norepinephrine receptors, including Venlafaxine and Mirtazapine. These are most used as second choice drugs or for people with mixed anxiety and depression.

All the anti-depressants other than direct stimulants have a most annoying weakness which is that while the side-effects may start almost immediately the therapeutic effect on depression takes about two weeks to kick in. We do not know exactly why there is a lag period. All these drugs work better if taken regularly and their effect is long term not day to day like Aspirin or Diazepam. Surprisingly we still do not know exactly how this important group of drugs work. Their effects on the mono-amine nerves may not be the whole story. Recent advances suggest that they can stimulate nerves to grow new connections, perhaps explaining why their onset of action is so delayed.

The site of action is presumed to be the gaps between nerve endings which produce monoamine neuro-transmitters and the receptors on the nerves with which they are communicating. This is a complex locality with several different receptor sub-types and feed-back systems. In addition the same receptor can have different results in different parts of the brain. This causes many of the side-effects though some side-effects can be useful. Sedation in the day is a problem if you drive cars or machinery but is welcome at night if your sleep is poor as is common in depression. Sedation is a major reason for choosing one drug over another with the SSRI's tending not to be sedative whereas Amitriptyline and Mirtazapine are. Weight change is another big factor in drug choice as some anti-depressants do cause weight gain which may not help your level of well-being. This effect is unpredictable for each individual and trying out different drugs may be necessary.

Anti-depressants are so called because of their main use in treating depressed mood. This may be a misnomer as they have several other uses. They can help in anxiety and panic, in obsessional states, and in impulse control, and eating disorders. Side effects can be used in bed-wetting and premature ejaculation and some types of pain can be helped. They increase our ability to deal with stress and perhaps this is why they are so popular with stress being the epidemic rather than depression.

As the antidepressant market is so large there are always new drugs being researched and developed. Scientists are also looking at other chemical pathways in the brain to see if better drugs can be found or at least drugs with fewer side-effects. One interesting new product is Agomelatine which has effects on the Melatonin pathways as well as Serotonin. It has a normalising effect on disturbed sleep patterns distinguishing it from most anti-depressants which make the pattern of sleep less normal by reducing REM sleep even if total sleep time is increased.

A most annoying difficulty with these drugs is that we are so poor at predicting who will respond to which drug and who will have side effects. Theoretically we can say that DNA underlies this variation between people but we do not yet know if the language of genetics will prove practical and useful. One reason why individuality is neglected lies in the statistical methods of medical research. To show a drug works you need to demonstrate for a large number of people that on average the group does better on this drug than another large group of people do on placebo or that it works as well as a proven drug. Showing it works for one person is irrelevant. Finding differences between types of people is difficult because firstly it takes even larger numbers of people for the statistics to be significant and secondly you do not know how best to group people into types.

How long is a course of anti-depressants?

The usual answer to this question is 6 months for a first serious depression because a depressive episode typically lasts a few months if untreated. Anti-depressants do not cure the illness in that they do not end the episode but reduce symptoms. If you stop the drug before the episode has ended you will find you are still depressed. Of course life is not that simple and other factors may change in your life. For example drugs might improve your mood enough for you to take more exercise, become more sociable and remind you of a better sleep routine and these changes should persist when the drug is stopped.

More difficult is how long to stay on drugs if you have had more than one episode. Here the evidence is strong that you risk having future periods of depression and staying on antidepressants for a longer time will reduce this risk. Unfortunately they only work when you take them. Having taken them for 6 months or a year does not in itself provide any on-going protection once you have stopped. If depression has become a long term part of your life you do need to look at psychological and life-style approaches. If you are reliant on drugs long term then be sure to find the best one for you with most benefit and least side-effects. This can be hard if on the one hand you are thankful and relieved to have found a drug that helps your mood but on the other hand you find the side-effects tough. Talk to your doctor about whether the side-effects are likely to reduce in time as some do and about possible dose reductions.

Thinking electric

Electro-convulsive Therapy (ECT) is the most powerful physical treatment for depression and raises some challenging questions. ECT is a very strange and to many people unacceptable treatment but it can jolt people out of the most severe states of depression, apparently ending the episode. The mechanics of this are unknown but there is an argument for preferring this over drug therapy which does not fundamentally end an episode so much as reduce symptoms and drugs have their own side effects. The case for ECT is much stronger where someone is so depressed as to be unable to look after basic needs and is too far gone to respond to talking therapy. Depression in its most severe form results in a person becoming mute and stuporose. ECT's place in moderate depression not responding to drugs is much less certain as a doctor biased towards biological treatment may not try hard enough with psychological therapies. Our culture is caught between its belief in biological physical therapies of which ECT is the strongest example and our natural fear of damaging the delicate structure of the brain. Shockingly ECT has some very dark chapters in its history where it has either been abused as a therapy or has been deliberately used to damage people. Our ambivalence is reflected in ECT being available in some developed countries but not others, in some US states but not others.

ECT works somehow through causing fits or convulsions in the brain. Theoretically it should be possible to have a similar effect using less power by applying magnetic fields rather than direct electric current. This Transcranial Magnetic Simulation therapy has been developed but so far does not seem to be as effective as ECT in treating depression. It is also being tried in migraine and neuropathic pain.

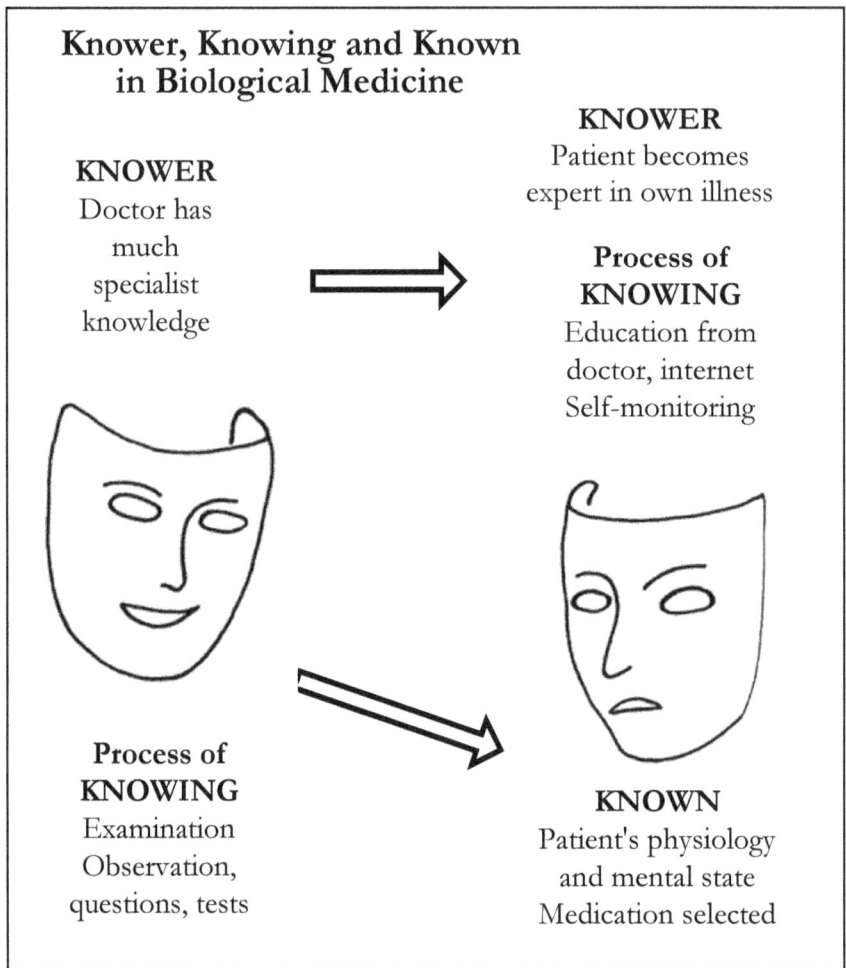

Knower, Knowing and Known in Biological Medicine

KNOWER
Doctor has much specialist knowledge

KNOWER
Patient becomes expert in own illness

Process of KNOWING
Education from doctor, internet
Self-monitoring

Process of KNOWING
Examination
Observation, questions, tests

KNOWN
Patient's physiology and mental state
Medication selected

Knowing enough

The risk in biological therapy is that the doctor has all the knowledge. Most patients do not know much neuro-physiology and are unlikely to want to know the intricacies of all their neuro-transmitters and receptor sub-types. You do not want to hear that you have some hard to describe physical tendency to depression which can only be managed by taking drugs whose mode of action is equally obscure. This is important because helplessness is an issue in depression. Especially when depression is a long-term problem you need to educate yourself and become more of a Knower, less an object of knowledge for your doctor.

For all chronic conditions such as diabetes or heart disease there is much more emphasis nowadays on self-management and education. Patients are encouraged to be more in the Knower role, to keep an eye on their own progress and to take positive action not just take pills. In depression a side benefit of this approach is that it increases your sense of self efficacy and reduces helplessness. You can learn about your medication – its timing, the importance of regularity, potential side-effects. Also useful are the other strategies to use alongside medication even if you are not entering into some other formal therapy. At a chemical level there is little point in taking medication if you are pounding your brain with depressants like alcohol. Attention to the simple strategies of exercise, diet and daily routine will also pay dividends both mentally and physically.

More than the objective

The objective study of the body, through medical science and through clinical testing, requires the addition of subjective study. As individuals and potential patients we experience our own bodies directly through our senses. With the refinement of consciousness our senses become more accurate. We can be more aware of what is life-supporting whether in terms of diet or exercise or daily routine. For example we should be aware of how much we need to eat to assuage our hunger without becoming overweight and how much rest and activity we need. Harmful substances should be less attractive to us even at the sensory level. In a state of perfect health our senses naturally support healthy desires and provide accurate feedback as to the effects of behaviour on our health. In the depressed state our natural ability to make healthy choices is reduced causing a vicious circle of deteriorating life-style and mood. This is why having prior education about healthy habits is so important.

As we see later in the book Natural Medicine places more value on training our senses and Vedic science goes well beyond biological science because of the primary place it gives to the field of consciousness itself. All animals and all of nature can be seen objectively to be based on the laws of nature in the Unified Field. Only man can experience this in his individual consciousness. This unique functioning of our mind is reflected in the size and complexity of our brain. It is the overall functioning of the brain that allows this. It is not simply due to an extra bit in the brain or some single chemical. If you dissect a human brain you do not find a special bit labelled consciousness or soul.

Every state of consciousness whether dreaming, sleeping, waking, being depressed or being enlightened has its parallel state of the physiology. Biological medicine tries to shift you from the depressed state to your usual level of mood but at present we only understand these states very partially at a chemical level.

Evidence for Drug Therapy in Depression

The effect of antidepressants varies greatly from one person to another. You might be lucky and have the magical result and feel 100% back to normal or you might strike out and feel nothing. Overall any particular drug works in around 2/3 of people who take it. That means they have a significant improvement in your depressive symptoms – not necessarily back to 100%. This is not a tremendous success rate. However if you fail on one drug you can try another and usually one from another chemical group would be picked. Then you could try a third. As you need to try each one for several weeks to give it a chance to work this can require patience but persistence can pay off. If your depression has been with you a long time and other methods have not worked or do not appeal then a period of experimenting with different drugs may be for you.

If you have no luck with three or four individual drugs then there is the choice of trying a combination of two anti-depressants or adding another type of drug. Using two anti-depressants is quite common though there is little clinical trial data to support this and side-effects become more likely. Nevertheless there are theoretical reasons for hope that a combined influence on your neuronal receptors may work. Adding a different type of drug we can choose from one of the Bipolar mood stabilising drugs or one of the anti-psychotic drugs. These have a role even for someone who does not have Bipolar or psychotic illness. Buspirone, an anti-anxiety drug is used especially with the SSRI's as an adjunctive therapy and may also help with some side effects. In any case if you are taking more than one drug closer monitoring by your doctor is indicated because of side effect risk and to make sure the doses are optimal.

Which people are comfortable with Drug Therapy?

Medication suits people who do not want to make the effort involved in psychological therapies. This may reflect not wanting to be the Knower. Plainly it can also reflect your depression reducing your energy to do anything. If depression is a longer term problem you need to challenge this reluctance to take more control.

Perhaps you are not comfortable with drugs and want to use psychological and life-style therapies but are so severely depressed that your doctor is advising anti-depressants. In this case you could see the drugs as a temporary or supportive strategy which allows you to recover enough energy and mood to make good use of the other methods. It is not good to be too comfortable with drug therapy as this makes you less likely to make other changes in your life. This is the same situation as with heart disease or diabetes.

Particularly the stimulant medicines are not good for people with addictive tendencies though they will be keen to choose them. Nor is it logical to take drugs for depression if you are currently taking chemicals that worsen or destabilise your mood such as alcohol and illegal drugs.

One indication for drug therapy is having a strong family history of depression and of relatives who have responded well to drugs. Even knowing which specific drugs is a useful guide as both therapeutic effects and side-effects have genetic influences. Drugs are obviously less attractive if you fear side-effects though trialling different medicines should minimise this problem.

Drugs can be combined with another therapy such as CBT. Even if you are convinced that your problem is mainly genetic and biological, the evidence is that other approaches will add benefit.

Summary

Anti-depressant drugs have become the commonest and standard treatment for depression and remain the focus of much research. This is despite them often causing side effects and often being only partially successful. Drugs are aimed at putting our brain chemistry into better balance. Other simpler methods look to rebalance our activity/rest levels and our sleep patterns.

The core biological disturbance in depression is elusive due to the brain's complexity so it is hard to see exactly what we are trying to rebalance. The stress hormone HPA axis is important. Our sleep pattern is also a marker for depression. While simple approaches such as exercise and daily routine address the body at a gross level, drugs target the fine level of our neuro-transmitters. This gives them a potentially powerful effect but also the risk of side-effects due to complexity.

Arguably the most powerful biological therapy is ECT yet we instinctively hesitate before applying such a shock to the brain. In many places we even legislate against it. We have no such qualms about giving mind-altering chemicals which so many of the population now take for long periods. Maybe our familiarity with the psychotropic effects of caffeine and alcohol allow us to tolerate this. Alcohol is one of the big untreated factors in the epidemic depression. Unfortunately it is easier for us to add more drugs than to stop the harmful ones.

It may be the nature of the depressed state that leads us to rely so much on anti-depressant drugs. We do not have the energy or initiative to make the effort and change our life-style or use psychological therapy. These drugs can be very useful for some but they are clearly not a complete or adequate answer to the epidemic of depression weighing our society down.

Key points from Biological Psychiatry

∞ Rest and activity are both important to our mood
∞ Physical health especially cardiovascular health is important for mental resilience
∞ Deeper levels of the physiology, like neuro-transmitters, are powerful but our knowledge is only partial

Challenge for Biological Psychiatry

We need to involve patients more in their own care rather than being passive recipients of medication and where medication is only partially successful other methods must be used. We need to find more effective and healthier ways of rebalancing our bodies and brain chemistry. Can we find a deeper more holistic level of the physiology which can be used to go beyond the partial success and side-effects of anti-depressants? Can biological scientists join physicists in recognising the Unified Field of natural law as the basis of the brain?

∞ Chapter 7 ∞
Harmony with Nature
Natural Medicine

There is a galaxy of Natural Medicine approaches. Some are traditional, some are bizarre, some are gentle, and some just frightening. It might have been hard to know if you need drugs, CBT or Psychoanalysis from mainstream psychiatry but it is even more difficult to pick from the smorgasbord of natural choices. Natural Medicine used to be on the fringe but has become ubiquitous despite the best efforts of Western Medicine to suppress it. Magazines and TV health programs are incomplete without some Yoga, aromas or massage.

Natural traditions emphasise the connection between man and nature with two of the important linkages being time and diet. The rhythms and cycles of nature are mirrored in our physiology and psychology. Balance is good and lack of synchrony causes illnesses. As we have seen modern physiological research is validating the crucial role of our circadian rhythm in depression. A modern urban life-style allows us to ignore the natural timing of day and night but unfortunately our bodies have evolved to be in harmony with the timing of the sun and our clocks are not as easy to reset as our smart-phones.

Food is the most material connection between body and environment. Our culture has progressed to having enough food, to having too much food, and now being diet crazy. Poor diet is another candidate for Agent Blue with the widespread use of junk foods. Alongside and within food are environmental toxins, chemicals we ingest unknowingly from air pollution and food additives, insecticides etc. There are so many of these their effects are hard to analyse but we do know they can interact with our hormone and transmitter systems. Indeed some of them are given to our farm animals precisely to affect their hormones.

Modern science analyses food in terms of chemical analysis: carbohydrates, fats, proteins, minerals and vitamins however there is surprisingly little scientific research on different food types for example as to which might be good for depression. There is a wealth of advice in natural systems and this is often tied to your specific body type and state of imbalance. Natural Medicine tends to see some foods, like herbs, as especially potent influences on our body.

Many natural schools consider themselves holistic. This term means a variety of things. Holistic may refer to the unity of man and nature or of mind and body. Imbalance is seen as a general change across the whole system rather than an isolated piece being sick. Holistic use of herbs could mean that that the intelligence of the whole herb is used not just an isolated chemical component. A holistic view of the body starts with the wholeness which is then seen as having different dimensions or aspects, rather than starting with parts like chemicals cells and organs which build up to make the body.

Energy levels and channels are another common pre-occupation of natural systems. Lack of energy or tiredness is one of the commonest symptoms seen in general medicine and of course in depression but modern medicine struggles to describe the physiological basis for this. Natural systems argue that the imbalance is too subtle to be tracked to an isolated part of the body.

The spectrum of natural approaches

The natural understandings of health cover the senses, energy levels and pathways, and the natural rhythms of life. The older systems like Traditional Chinese Medicine (TCM) and Ayur Veda from India have many departments whereas some newer ideas concentrate on one idea like Iridology or Reflexology.

Taste and smell relate to food and aromas, sight to light and colour therapy, touch to massage and manipulation, and hearing to the use of music, chanting, whale song and other sounds. Natural cycles have been mentioned as important in depression including daily, monthly and seasonal patterns. Energy levels are seen as primary in some systems as they power the body's healing efforts, not just being a secondary result of health or illness. Energy pathways are described in several major ways with special interest in the spine and central energy centres as well as peripheral lines in the body and limbs. These may be subject to pressure, needles, massage, specific postures and manipulation.

Modern science does not recognise most of the energy patterns but is coming to appreciate the role of biological rhythms. The importance of food and the digestive system is also more acknowledged and the gut has been found to have much more of its own nervous system and communication network than previously thought. Emotions may not just be felt in our internal organs but also generated from them. Imbalanced digestion and gut bacteria can certainly produce an excess of chemicals in the body such as inflammatory cytokines which affect mood.

Constitutional types and influences

The analytical approach of modern science is fairly recent. For most of human history we have had a more holistic view of ourselves and our place in the natural world. In the Ayur Vedic system of India and in TCM there are five elements and for much of European history we had four humours. Possibly one was lost in transit across the Middle East. These general factors can be used to describe both our individual health and the environment. Weather, geography and food all have influences on how we feel but have been hard to analyse at a chemical level. The apparently simplistic perspective of a holistic system is easier to relate to.

Whereas neuro-transmitters are hard to link to our everyday life natural systems have factors with familiar qualities like hot/cold, wet/dry. If your constitution has a cold character then cold weather, environment or food will push you further in that direction. Excessive or imbalanced cold plus dryness pushes in the Melancholic direction, while cold plus damp goes to the Phlegmatic side. Changes in the seasons can easily be factored in to suggest diets which balance the seasonal influences on your constitution. Such simple ideas may seem absurd in contrast to the scientific exactitude of modern science but if you look at all the chemical names on the back of your morning cereal packet and cross reference this with the bewildering advice from all the magazine diet columns can we say that modern science is that precise and helpful? Certainly in the treatment of depression it has not yet given us much regarding diet.

A basic understanding of the elements in one's constitution is learned quite easily once you have chosen a natural system. Self-knowledge here means knowledge of your body's tendencies, its strengths and weaknesses and how to monitor them. Such learning is especially useful for remaining in balance. In very general terms diet, herbs, and routine are used to remain in balance with expert advice sought when you have drifted too far out of line. The more developed systems like Ayur Veda and TCM have very sophisticated understandings of the physiology and of herbal medicine and their pharmacologies are as complex as that of modern medicine.

Energy levels

The vital energy that we experience has various names in different systems: *chi*, *prana*, life-force etc. You know when it is strong and in depression it is usually on the fainter side. Depression occurring in old age is more difficult to treat and one explanation is that this life-force is weaker in our older years so there is less energy around to balance or redirect.

Chronic fatigue is so common now as to have its own diagnosis. The modern science analysis has not been of great assistance as no single villain has been found to shoot down with a magic bullet. Various abnormalities have been implicated in the immune system or viral infections or stress responses. Most sufferers feel predominantly physical symptoms of tiredness and exhaustion. They are very resistant to being labelled as depressed which is a commentary on the continued stigma of mental illness. Whatever the original cause the syndrome is perpetuated by vicious circles of less activity, less stamina, and disturbed routines. Helplessness and low self-esteem and social withdrawal may also add their burdens.

The way out of chronic fatigue from modern rehabilitation is basically to increase your activity level slowly and gradually. This is little different to anyone who wishes to become more fit. Rest is also important but not so much rest as to prevent your training regime making progress.

Conditions like chronic fatigue and depression are prime candidates for Natural Medicine because modern medicine has incomplete answers. The modern description is also confusing as "depression" sounds like a psychological illness but the common therapy is a physical one, medication. Especially when symptoms seem very physical people may naturally seek a better sounding diagnosis and look to another system of medicine.

First do no harm

The simplest form of Natural Medicine is to stop doing what is unhealthy. This should be a basic part of any doctor's advice but it is often missed or down-played. Either we as doctors are too pessimistic about our patients changing their behavior or we are too guilty about our own high levels of alcohol intake. Alcohol is a main culprit as it is a direct depressant to the brain. This can give temporary happiness as it suppresses our worries but you pay the next day. As well as depressing the mood alcohol suppresses the higher functions of the brain like self-monitoring, decision making, moral reason, and future planning. These are just the abilities you actually need to plan your recovery from depression. Alcohol also brings its own secondary problems as your relationships and work and maybe police record deteriorate giving you more reasons to be depressed.

Some of the damage from alcohol reverses quickly when you stop drinking which will be encouraging but if you have drunk much and regularly the wait will be many months for full recovery. This is how long the neural pathways take to re-establish them-selves. If you have done extensive damage to those you love then you are faced with a potentially even longer period of seeking forgiveness and re-conciliation.

Stimulant drugs such as crack or cocaine are different but not better for you. The immediate effect is much greater in terms of being elated but by the same token they are rapidly addictive and personality changing, life destroying.

At the milder end of the drug spectrum we have caffeine. This is worse for anxiety than depression but it does destabilise circadian rhythms. Caffeine intake is increasing with large doses available in energy drinks. Needing coffee on the morning to get going does not seem too evil but it is a sign that your sleep cycle is out of balance. Frequently needing coffee could be a warning sign that you are stressed and in danger of becoming depressed. Stopping caffeine would test this out and many people are more addicted than they think.

Exercise

One of the major advances in the treatment of depression in the last generation has been the recognition that exercise is good for your mood. It helps the body distinguish night from day and improves your sleep. At a chemical level serotonin is increased and endorphins released. Gradually increasing exercise improves energy levels. Any form of exercise seems to work as long as you do it regularly. Probably less effort is needed to improve your mood than to radically change your cardiovascular health. 15-30 minutes moderate exercise most days is generally recommended, ideally daily but your mood will not flat-line if you miss a day.

Exercise may also help you get out and spend time with others if you keep fit in a group. As with other life-style changes it allows you some executive control over your depression doing something for yourself to improve the mood. Rather than seeing reduced activity as an inevitable result of depression we can view exercise as a positive escape strategy. Making such a change can be analysed as a behavioral change or as needing a cognitive change to enable it. However the underlying cultural growth making physical exercise an expected part of a healthy life is also helpful.

Exercise is obviously more important for those of us who have been inactive. For this group, regular exercise is as effective as anti-depressants for mild to moderate levels of depression.

You are what you eat

Diet has become a huge topic of debate and advertising, so much as to become a stress in itself. We are constantly being called to decide if our body is a temple built of pure materials or a warehouse for junk and obesity is the largest physical health issue of our time. We have not yet met the challenge of living with more than enough food being available in developed countries. Our physiologies did not evolve in this environment so we have to use our intellects to manage our basic drive to eat. Pretty much every suggestion has been made and has a book, video, and workshop to be bought: no carbohydrates, no fat, low protein, fasting, reindeer meat, and a multitude of super-foods.

Biochemistry identifies vitamins, minerals and co-enzymes which sound great. It would be very convenient if depression and other problems responded to taking a few supplements. This hope has spawned a multi-billion dollar industry supplying these little extras. It is so much easier to add something to your diet than to take anything away. Unfortunately if you are eating a mixed diet in modern times there is little evidence you will be helped much by taking supplements.

Vitamin D may be worth looking at in depression and is the subject of on-going research. Vitamin D levels are sub-optimal in many people in the USA and there is increasing evidence that levels are low in depression. There may be a bit of chicken-and-egg here as depressed people go out less and get less sunlight. However Vitamin D is implicated in neurotransmitter function and neural growth so it is worth keeping an eye on. Folate has also been found to be protective of developing depression in some studies.

Fish oil despite the smell has become popular for health and there is some evidence it has a role in stabilising Bipolar disorder, less evidence yet for use in other forms of depression.

Herbs are used in cooking and also as traditional medicines in all parts of the world, most systems tailoring the herbs to types of imbalance in the mind and body. In our modern way we like to tie treatments to illnesses or symptoms. St John's Wort is a well-recognised treatment for depression and randomised clinical trials show it to be as effective as antidepressants in mild to moderate illness. It has fewer side-effects and is relatively cheap. In countries like Germany with strong traditions of herbal medicine it is the commonest medicine for depression. In the USA over 4 million people use it in a year.

Herbal medicines do tend to have fewer side effects but they should not be seen as chemically inert. St John's Wort does interact with some modern medicines including altering blood levels of some antidepressants so it is better not to mix them. Probably St John's Wort affects our neuro-transmitter or neuro-endocrine systems but this may not be the best way of understanding its mechanism of action.

One curious fact about our body is that there are more bacterial cells in it than human and most of these are in the digestive tract. The gut and the brain are well connected both by the autonomic nervous system and the blood stream. The gut wall cells and the bacteria produce many chemicals which are neuro-transmitters, precursors of neuro-transmitters, or are neuro-modulators. It is known that anxiety and depression are associated across the life span with dysfunction of the digestive system and it is likely this is a two-way relationship. A disturbed mood often leads to changes in your digestion and long term a disturbed digestion almost certainly influences mood. Research is on-going into whether ensuring a good balance of bacteria in the gut through the use of pro-biotics can protect us from depression.

Jane

Jane had plenty of reasons for feeling depressed. Her second husband had just upped and offed, her teen-age daughter was giving her grief and she had been stressed by a breast cancer scare. Despite all this she did not think she should be so down, as in the past she had coped better with life's problems. She was 46 years old and had always been a hard worker, currently managing a successful clothing store. She did not want to go down the anti-depressants route and had already done some positive thinking courses in the past so she looked around for some Natural Medicine. She had been to an osteopath in the past who did her back some good but that seemed OK now. Massage was not really her thing but she was into aromas and herbs.

A friend recommended an herbal therapist who gave her St John's Wort, B Vitamins, and Lavender oil for bed-time. She felt good about using these and did have benefits to her mood and stress levels. She had some informal counselling from the therapist regarding her relationships but this was more by way of ventilation and she already really knew what she had to do in this area of life. She was given some general advice on healthy food but she knew most of this as well. She was not a great alcohol drinker but had increased her coffee intake from one to four a day. She agreed to go back to one or ideally swop for herb tea.

Would she have been as successful with a modern anti-depressant? Possibly she would have done well but her depression was not severe and she did benefit from the herbal medicine with no side-effects. The coffee reduction can be significant. She had no prior history of much rhythm disturbance such as insomnia or PMS but caffeine does affect the circadian rhythm which is so often deranged in depression. Her choice of herbal medicine over a modern medicine reflects a wide-spread feeling that natural medicine is best, as long as it works.

Using our senses

Space does not allow us to look at every natural approach in detail. Most forms of Natural Medicine can be organised according to the five senses. The senses are how we relate to the natural world and are the obvious pathways to use in the natural approach to health. In modern times some of our senses have been overloaded, some deprived, and some distorted. Perhaps here we shall find more candidates for Agent Blue.

Hearing

Music has a remarkable effect on our mood and we choose different tracks to suit the occasion whether we are running, relaxing, driving or setting up a romantic evening. The sounds of our environment are influential though we might not think of this in the realm of therapy. One of the greatest environmental changes in the recent times has been the increase in noise levels that we live with. Machines are everywhere whirring, clanking, grinding and beeping. This could well be a factor in modern levels of stress and depression. Certainly for city folk the peace of the country-side is found to be healing in itself. It is no coincidence that the predominant music of our age is fast and loud trying to boost us over our low mood. At the extreme all-night parties combine loud stimulating music and stimulating recreational drugs to give a temporary kick to your mood. Possibly you might get the paradoxical benefit of sleep deprivation but the general experience the next day is of a hang-over. If you keep track of what music you are choosing it can tell you about your mood.

There are specific therapies which use sounds designed to have healthy results. This is usually a relaxing effect and a variety of natural sounds are used such as flowing water, breaking waves, rustling leaves and bird-song all of which would have been more part of our sound environment in the past. Whale song is popular though less easy to argue as a part of our ancestral experience. Chanting is another option and is often tied to a specific religious or indigenous tradition. The goals here may be as much spiritual as physical.

Sight

Just as the volume of sound is increasing our eyes are subjected to a staggering number of images. We are competing with each other as to who can see the most web-pages per minute. TV and our electronic devices are saving us the bother of having to imagine anything in our mind's eye. The screen conjures up pictures and videos for us and the speed with which we switch from one image to another is unprecedented in evolutionary terms. Whether this is good for us or harmful remains to be seen. There is evidence that the rapid seeking of new experience, which is mainly visual, becomes an addiction with short term rewards at the expense of deeper thought and it mutes our higher executive functions of self-monitoring and planning.

Advice on colour is everywhere for make-up, clothing and interior design. The colour of our rooms certainly does affect our mood as does the amount of overall light. Repainting your house might seem like an extreme therapy for depression but if you live and work in dark gloomy places you should at least get out more.

Light therapy has been noted to have a strong role in Seasonal Affective Disorder. There is a relationship between sunlight exposure and Vitamin D production. Getting outside tends to be associated with exercise, social contact, or being in greener pastures all of which are beneficial. Light therapy can also be much more subtle. Some natural systems see the body as having other levels of energy and intelligence including the "light body". Light therapy is used to interact at this level. This is beyond the analysis of modern medicine but does appeal to some.

Touch

While our hearing and sight are over-stimulated touch may be missing from our lives. The nourishing touch of other people has become problematic. Our sexual desires and fears have come to dominate social interaction to the point where any touch between adults has become risky in the work-place. Contact between adults and children is even more dangerous. If you do not live in a relationship or family where touch is OK and available then your only source of physical contact may be the unwelcome crush in the commuter train. Domestic pets can have a role here providing a companion who is safe to stroke.

In a culture short on touch it is not surprising that touching therapies should flourish. Massage is widely available and has an immediate relaxing effect. Massage may be directed at the muscles and relieving tension, at increasing blood flow to internal organs, at stimulating specific energy points, or at more subtle layers of the body. Non-contact aura massage operates on an external but subtle level while other schools use the refined senses of the therapist to sense what is happening at deeper levels within the body. The research support for massage is more for anxiety and stress than depression. Reduction of the stress-related hormones can be seen and chronic stress is associated with the development of depression.

The flourishing sex industry also relates to lack of touch though with a particular focus regarding what sort of touch. Loneliness is a major factor in depression and sexual frustration is a part of this. Unfortunately our relationships are much too complex and multi-level for the sex trade to be a complete therapy though arguably it is natural.

At the more refined end of the market Yoga postures or *asanas* have been widely used for stress and anxiety which are common factors or antecedents to depression. The *asanas* have an effect on mechanical flexibility and muscular relaxation. At other levels they stimulate nervous and vascular pathways which are understood either in modern anatomical terms or as more subtle energy lines. Breathing exercises from the Yoga tradition have been shown to be of benefit in depression. This may be a combination of their effect on soothing anxiety and stress and their influence on positive energy or prana levels. Yoga is so popular that several schools are now widespread. Hatha Yoga is a more straight-forward approach. Vinyasa uses more breathing techniques or coordination with postures. Bikram is the hot Yoga making you sweat and purify the body.

Acupuncture has an elaborate map of energy points and lines through the body. Blockages and imbalances are diagnosed and corrected by points being massaged or needled. TCM would not see depression as a unitary diagnosis but as arising from a number of possible causes. This makes research more difficult but there are some studies showing an effect of Acupuncture in depression.

The spine and spinal cord link the brain to the body and its peripheral nerves. There are many therapies involving massage or manipulation of the spine. Theories range from the mechanical view of the bones and joints to the finer energy flows within. Osteopathy and Chiropractic are well established treatments for spinal problems which do not find solutions in modern medicine. Cranial osteopathy is a development that aims to improve circulation of cerebrospinal fluid in and around the brain and spinal cord. As with most refined techniques this depends on the advanced perception and influence of the therapist so a bit more faith is required.

Smell

Aroma therapy has become very widely accepted in Western culture. It appeals as being non-invasive, gentle, and pleasant. We all like good smells and this most primitive of senses is well wired into the emotional circuits of our brain. Because our common experience tells us smells can have positive emotional effect we have not been very demanding of scientific studies. There are some studies, again more for anxiety than depression, showing benefit but the overwhelming diffusion of aroma therapy into popular culture goes way beyond the scientific evidence. Sandalwood and sweet orange are commonly used in depression. Others are used in the frequent companion problems of anxiety and insomnia.

Taste

We have already looked at some aspects of food and at St John's Wort the commonest herbal anti-depressant. Other herbs recommended for depression include Ginseng, Liquorice, Fennel, Kava and Holy Basil. The evidence for their effectiveness is once again mainly for the stress and anxiety components.

Alcohol and coffee provide only brief relief and have long-term disadvantages for depression. Tea on the other hand is gathering good evidence for at least protecting against the chance of becoming depressed. Green tea appears to be more effective than black tea.

There are many suggestions as to foods that might help depression but not much evidence. Some foods are linked to biochemical ideas. For example foods like chick-peas which contain tryptophan which is a serotonin precursor have been promoted but lack of tryptophan is not likely to be a rate limiting step for serotonin production in the brain. Aspartame, an artificial sweetener, may impede serotonin function. Everybody's favourite is dark chocolate which increases endorphins but this may only be a temporary effect. Most natural systems recognise that people with different constitutions need different diets to stay balanced rather than promoting individual foods as anti-depressants for all.

Developed countries have more than enough food available and we have not managed this glut very well. Food technology has been more aimed at selling food than promoting health. One casualty of this trend has been our ability to use the natural sense of taste. Processed food is so laced with additives and flavours that taste is not a good guide. Many people now grow up to believe that if they do like the taste of something it must be bad for them. Eating more natural and less processed food is part of a solution and you may have to retrain your sense of taste.

If you are addicted to a drug you will miss it if not taken. Your sense of taste tells you to drink alcohol, or consume stimulants. Their taste (or smell) has become tied to the pleasant short-term effects. At a less extreme level you eat comforting food for brief pleasure despite their longer term effects on your weight and health. Clearly we do develop bad habits which need replacing. We suffer from a biased menu of foods being commonly eaten which has too much sweet, salty and sour food and not enough other tastes. This is one explanation of why we keep over-eating to try to satisfy ourselves. A more balanced diet would be more fulfilling.

Many depressed people over-eat and then put on weight which then lowers self-esteem with seasonal depression usually being of this type. Unfortunately most modern anti-depressants tend to increase your weight which would obviously be more useful if weight has been lost. Some severe depressions are marked by loss of appetite and weight and this is a significant sign of your needing help.

Time

Nature is structured round the cycles of the day, the months and the seasons. As with taste our sense of what time it is has been reduced, in this case by our access to electric lights and heating. Our internal world has similar cycles to the environment but they are weakened when we have poor cues to remind us. The pattern of depression is often worse at certain times of the month for women and varies seasonally if you live far enough away from the equator.

It is well-known that depression is commoner in women and there are many possible explanations rhythm instability being one. The increased frequency of depression occurs during the ages when women have active menstrual cycles. The menstrual cycle does affect other rhythms particularly the daily rhythm and makes it less stable.

Modern analysis of circadian rhythm focuses on sleep and light/dark changes. A Natural Medicine approach will look more into timing of eating and activity within the day as well as sleep times. Scientific analysis does show clear sub-cycles within the daily rhythm. The body remembers what your schedule is and your meal will be better digested if it is taken at the usual time than if you spring a pizza on your system in the middle of the night.

Richard and the natural health consultant

In this incarnation Richard goes down the natural road. He had heard bad things about drug side-effects and thought he might be too intelligent for CBT. He knew his life-style was not the best and had an inkling that there was a stronger healthier Richard inside waiting to be revealed. He did not want to go for anything too invasive like needles, enemas or chakra balancing. To start with he decided to have what he thought of as a tune-up. He saw a Holistic Health therapist who advertised analysis of diet, exercise and life-style. He had heard good reports about her which was important as he had no idea what her qualifications meant.

He was concerned the consultation might be a bit like going to confession but was reassured by her positive attitude. You are naturally healthy and being healthy is easier than being out of balance. He had to agree that his current life was not easy. She challenged him as to whether he wanted to make some small incremental adjustments or take larger strides towards a healthy life. Was he a man or a mouse? Somehow he agreed to make some serious changes.

She placed a good deal of emphasis on his daily routine. He was getting up in the morning well after the sun and going to bed much too late. The best sleep starts around 10pm not midnight. He was not getting enough sleep in the week and then having a longer alcohol assisted sleep on the weekend. Certainly he did not show the obvious symptom of good sleep, waking up feeling refreshed. His bed-time in the week was late as he was either working or watching TV and he also ate a large meal quite late in the evening.

His new routine was to eat more at lunch time and a lighter meal earlier in the evening. As the Behaviorist suggested she also pointed out the benefits of not working or watching TV in the late evening. Once he was going to bed earlier he would be waking earlier and have time for some exercise in the morning. Richard had never been greatly into sports and did not see himself running or going to the gym before work. His school was too far to walk to but not too far for a cycle ride. This is something he had enjoyed doing when he was a school-boy and appealed to him as an outward signal that he was creating a new and livelier Richard.

This therapist was quite tough on coffee and alcohol. Coffee might pick you up but it stressed your internal rhythms. Alcohol was just a poison wrecking your metabolism, your sleep and your mood. Richard was OK committing to less coffee and phasing this out but alcohol was harder. He would try for none in the week and a limit per session at the weekend. The therapist assured him that as he became healthier his body would crave artificial supports less.

She focussed less on the details of his diet as he was clearly not too interested and probably not a great cook. She emphasised the amount and timing of food and just suggested more fresh fruit and veg. Nor did she want to overload him with other elements of Natural Medicine. She gave him an aroma to use at night if he had trouble falling asleep and recommended he have a full body massage at the weekend for a few weeks to help his body release stress and recover it-self.

Richard did begin to feel physically stronger and soon acclimatised to the new food timing. Importantly he felt he was *rebuilding himself at least his physiology. He was aware he needed to make some changes in his mental approach to important areas of life but was putting these off till he felt healthier. As his sleep improved his energy picked up. He was less drained at weekends and was more able to use time to think about his options and discuss these with his girl-friend rather than just collapse into alcohol-induced rest.*

Knower Knowing and Known in Natural Medicine

The essence of natural methods can be captured in a language which is natural and so is easier for the patient to understand and own. A natural description of our tendencies and the influences of the environment uses the familiar language of our senses. How does something taste or smell? What do we feel in our body? This contrasts with the language of modern science which often struggles to be understood by doctors let alone the public.

As a patient you are more involved in your assessment as your likes and dislikes, your physical reactions are involved. Once you are better informed about your constitution and state of balance then you are more empowered to make changes in terms of life-style and specific diets, aromas, and other behaviors. You may be asked to monitor yourself in terms of how your feelings and desires change. As your senses refine your appreciation of what is good for you will change and unhealthy choices lose their appeal.

In general Natural Medicine tends to increase the use of the patient as part of the Knowing process and their becoming a Knower of their own health. The Known is their state of balance and also the factors in life that put them in or out of balance.

There are yet some magicians in natural traditions whose knowledge remains hidden. For some of us the wise specialist is attractive. We believe there are deeper more powerful levels to life but we do not have the time or energy to learn about them so we prefer to leave that to the mysterious expert.

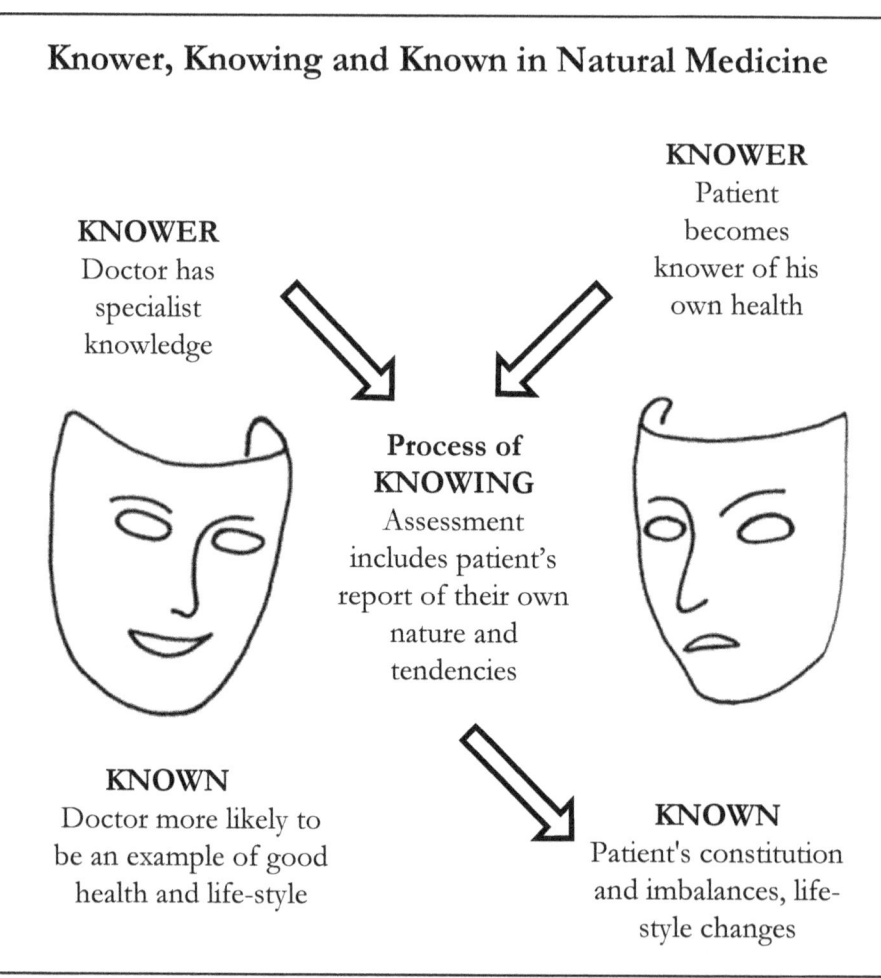

As in modern medicine milder imbalances are easier to take responsibility for one-self and more severe problems are more suitable for specialised knowledge or active intervention. Natural traditions are less known for extreme procedures such as surgery (though the earliest treatise on surgery is in the Ayur Vedic literature). However there are many treatments applied by a therapist including massage, acupuncture, manipulation, light therapy, not to mention enemas and other purifying processes. In all of these the patient is a passive participant even if the result is hoped to be the patient becoming purer and so in closer touch with their state of health.

Effectiveness of Natural Medicine in Depression

There are some stand-out natural therapies which are well evidenced: St John's Wort, exercise, and stopping alcohol. There is increasing evidence for correcting your daily routine, for green tea, and Yoga. For most natural approaches there are very keen therapists and self-reports of benefit from clients but either little or contradictory evidence from clinical trials. There is more evidence for effects on anxiety and insomnia and stress than on depressed mood though these are often a part of the depressive syndrome.

Acupuncture for example has some great studies showing effects as good as SSRI drugs and increases in GDNF a neuroprotective protein which is low in depression. However there are problems with the research. Can we really have a placebo comparison group for the process of Acupuncture? Having "blinded" patients or staff is very hard. The results from Asia seem better than in the West possibly due to reporting bias – that is not reporting negative results.

Similar issues exist for many other natural therapies. On the other hand many natural therapies do have years even centuries of experience and it can be argued that knowledge does not survive that long unless it has some value. Some systems of Natural Medicine do not see depression as a category or specific illness as the underlying causes are multiple. Natural interventions may not expect to have sudden effects but rather move you gradually towards a better state of health. This means research takes longer and is more prone to interference from other influences. Modern medical research is rather keen on the more manageable eight week trials. As with Psychoanalysis, the deeper natural therapies look at each individual and their special needs. This undermines our usual research methods which aggregate people together and find their average improvement.

Politics is another barrier to research into Natural Medicine as Western Medicine has tried to side-line and discredit Natural Medicine. Financially it is a competitor and its paradigms are hard to comprehend for doctors, especially specialists, trained in the modern science approach. Natural approaches have been kept out of medical schools and research institutes. This has begun to change but there remains a big difference between the public view that there is much to gain from Natural Medicine and its reluctant acceptance by mainstream Western Medicine.

Which people are comfortable with Natural Medicine?

Everyone will find some level of Natural Medicine acceptable. Life-style changes are obviously a good thing with the major barriers being lack of motivation when depressed and the seduction of the easy option of taking drugs. Some will prefer the physical bias of Natural Medicine though if you really need to talk a problem through there may be no avoiding this. One of the less recognised forms of Natural Medicine is going to the hair-dresser which is an important part of many women's routine. Surveys show that for many women their hair-dresser is the person with whom they are most likely to discuss emotional problems. The relaxed and safe environment with some gentle head massage provides an excellent space.

The wide spectrum of natural methods allows us to choose according to our taste. You can find specialists with arcane knowledge just as hidden as in Western Medicine. You can be a passive object of therapy and have strange things done to you. On the other side we can take responsibility for changing our habits, diet and exercise. Which sensory modality you prefer depends on your constitution. Health spas are flooding the market now and these go for a variety of senses especially touch, temperature, smell, and taste if you are dining in. Spas offering detox regimes also appeal to people who like to indulge and pay the price afterwards rather than keeping in health credit all the time.

You can usually combine modern and Natural Medicine and many do this. Even if you are unfortunate enough to need the tough end of modern medicine, such as cancer therapies, natural methods my help you at least in coping with the stress and side-effects of your treatment. For depression it is important not to mix natural and modern drugs. It is also good to have a consistent treatment strategy. As in heart disease it is fine to address more than one factor causing depression but make sure your efforts are not in conflict with eachother. If one therapist is convincing you that your serotonin activity needs the boost from an SSRI while another is persuading you that modern medicine is blocking the flow of energy through your chakras then it may be time to visit the hairdresser and discuss your options.

The non-verbal techniques of Natural Medicine may be very suitable for people who have experienced trauma. The usual modern psychology therapy for trauma has been talking about it, re-experiencing or re-integrating difficult memories. This is hard when memories are extreme or you come from a sub-culture when talking is not the usual route to recovery. Non-verbal therapy like massage are welcomed in this situation and can work on the stress stored in the skin and muscles and provide a more immediate form of care and reassurance.

Natural Medicine is also seen as a path to a higher state of balance in the body and of enlightenment in the mind. Initially we would address the grosser forms of imbalance by stopping harmful habits. Then we refine our diet and life-style and detox accumulated stresses. Applied therapy will move from overcoming blocks to balancing energy flows or opening up more subtle channels. Some approaches are designed to work on a finer level of energy or light or the quantum level. In such systems it is best to have an idea of which level you are at before planning your next steps. For such a journey it is definitely better to stick to one system and learn its theory. Scientific evidence for much of the finer work will not be available and you will have to rely more on your own self-assessment and experience.

Summary

Natural Medicine offers a multitude of approaches to harmonise ourselves with the natural environment. Some of the most useful are the simplest: daily routine, exercise, and diet. There are specific treatments such as St John's Wort which are well evidenced but many widely used therapies are supported more by their long tradition of use than by modern research. Some advice will be obvious like drinking less alcohol but more surprisingly drinking green tea may protect against depression.

Beyond the general advice there are many different systems offering individualised analysis and guidance. To gain the most from these you should learn and take ownership of the knowledge to best integrate it in your life. Much natural advice, particularly regarding life-style, will be compatible with modern therapies whether Cognitive Therapy or medication but we do need to be careful of mixing medications or using extreme diets. As depression is usually multi-factorial it seems reasonable to take more than one treatment approach.

Natural medicine pays more attention than modern psychiatry to promoting positive health and staying in balance with some systems offering a vision of higher states of mental and physical health.

Key Points from Natural Medicine

∞ The laws of nature are common to the body and the environment and a natural language can be found to describe them

∞ Synchrony of internal and external cycles is disturbed in depression

∞ Our senses can guide us to healthy choices if they are properly cultivated

∞ Deeper levels of energy and intelligence can be located in the body

Challenge for Natural Medicine

Traditions of Natural Medicine hold much complex and subtle knowledge. As in modern medicine there is still a tendency for deeper and specialist knowledge to stay in the mind of the therapists. There is a belief that the laws of nature underlie the environment and the individual but these laws are not necessarily easy to know. Can a natural method be found to harness the potential of our own minds so that we can have the laws of nature not only balanced in our body but lively in our own consciousness?

Many traditions do not say much about the nature of the mind as they focus on diet, herbs, massage etc. without a big mental component. Often the emphasis is on the mind being affected by the physical body and life-style though many do hold that the attention of the mind has a positive effect. Maharishi Ayur Veda holds consciousness to be central to health and this is discussed in the next chapter.

∞ Chapter 8 ∞
The Science of Life
Maharishi Ayur Veda

Ayur Veda is the traditional medicine from the Indian sub-continent and is the oldest recorded system of Natural Medicine. Regrettably it was suppressed by the British during their period of rule but has revived itself since their departure. Ayur Veda has a detailed understanding of the structure and function of the body which uses quite different principles to that of Western biochemistry. Maharishi Ayur Veda (MAV) describes the rediscovery of consciousness as the basis not only of the mind but also of the body and indeed the environment. Maharishi Mahesh Yogi worked with Vedic experts to show that all branches of Vedic knowledge are unified through the field of consciousness and this is particularly important for Ayur Veda – the science of life.

MAV contains knowledge about consciousness as the fundamental field of life and techniques to utilise this domain. It describes the basic qualities of the physiology to enable us to understand our constitution and how our lives keep us in balance. Self-referral is a cornerstone of MAV. This is seen in the practice of meditation and in the use of our senses to guide healthy behaviour, especially diet and daily routine. While MAV includes the use of material tools, such as food and herbal medicines, their value is seen at the level of their intelligence which interacts with our own consciousness. Natural rhythms are central to synchronising our physiology with the environment. All these elements, mental tendencies, physical body and the outside world are described in a simple language based on the three Doshas.

Doshas

Western medicine emphasises individual diseases and their specific treatments. MAV starts with health as a state of balanced wholeness. Our constitution has three fundamental attributes called Doshas: Vata, Pitta, and Kapha. We all have our own mixture of these three. This simple approach can be used by anyone and there is much more detail available for those who wish to become experts. For example it is helpful just to know how strong your digestion is and how to keep this in balance. In fine detail there are 15 stages of digestion and metabolism – more than most of us want to know.

Knowing your constitution tells you in which direction you are more likely to become unbalanced. The Doshas can be used to understand the influence of different foods, of the seasons and time of day, and different types of activity. We know that everyone has different preferences for food and exercise which reflect their constitution which is why there is no miracle diet for everybody and no single exercise video for all. MAV does contain much detail but it is the overall tendencies of the body and the general principles of health that dominate.

Vata relates to movement, having qualities of lightness, dryness, airiness. People with strong Vata tend to be thinner, faster and more variable. Their sleep and appetite are lighter and less regular. They are more prone to anxiety. Pitta relates to heat, metabolism and transformation. Pitta types are sharper and more exact with strong appetite. They are more prone to irritability if out of balance. Kapha relates to the structure of the body and Kapha people have strong bones and teeth, thick hair and a happy appearance. They are slower and steadier in their routines and their mood. Out of balance their tendency is to less action and slowed thinking.

As psychiatry has becomes more specialised like every other department we have invented dozens of different diseases. Our diagnostic systems look somewhat like cheap restaurant menus with long lists of items not obviously connected together. There is now a movement to look at the more fundamental modes of disturbance. This is evident in the field of mood disorder where instability of mood is seen as a useful concept which underlies a number of disorders such as Cyclothymia (a tendency to mood swings which is less severe than Bipolar illness), Atypical Depression, and Borderline Personality Disorder. This concept clearly reflects Vata aggravation and the high prevalence of these disorders in Western society parallels its strong tendency towards Vata imbalance.

This is not to say that just three groups of people who have three sorts of depression. We are all a mixture and even if you are very strongly of one Dosha, another Dosha might go out of balance. Knowing your constitutional balance tells you which imbalance is most likely for you and also which influences in your daily routine of environment will push you out of balance.

How the Doshas describe depression varies according to the type of depression. Vata pushes us towards anxious depression, Pitta towards irritable mood and Kapha towards lethargy but more than one Dosha or sub-Dosha is often involved. For example one part of Pitta, Sadhaka, relates to the heart and emotions and it can affect a part of Kapha, Tarpaka, which coordinates and stabilises the mind-heart relationship. In turn the part of Vata, Prana, that relates to mental energy and stability can be affected. General advice on meditation, routine and diet will help the balance of the Doshas with more specific foods, herbs or aromas targeting subdivisions of the Doshas.

Rhythms and Routines

Daily routine and biological rhythms are hard to study in modern science because so many measurements need to be made to establish a pattern. We know that these rhythms are often disturbed in mental illness and that this is not necessarily the consequence of illness. Disturbed rhythms are themselves important triggers and if disturbed may be a mechanism underlying illness, particularly with respect to depression. MAV sees rhythms as crucial to maintain balance just as a gyroscope maintains its position by rotating. These range from the pulse to breathing to the 90 minute hormonal pattern to daily, monthly and seasonal rhythms. Typically the rhythms travel from the influence of Kapha to Pitta and then to Vata.

Regularity of routines is particularly important to keep Vata in balance as Vata is the common cause of rhythm problems. One insight from MAV missing from modern medicine is that rhythms are linked or synchronised in health. If one rhythm is out of balance

– for example the monthly or menstrual cycle, then it is worth making your daily routine very regular as this may stabilise the monthly cycle.

Times of year and times of day all have their Dosha influences. Pitta is stronger around the middle of the day and middle of the night, also in the summer-time. If you are Pitta in nature you might notice that if you do not get to bed around 10 to 10:30pm you seem to pick up in energy and also in appetite looking for that mid-night snack. Unfortunately this appetite is misplaced. At this time of day it is the internal metabolism of the body that is active but this does not want to deal with more food intake. Getting to bed earlier is healthier and this is especially true if you are vulnerable to depression. One reason our culture is so biased to rhythm imbalance is that we have developed a whole sub-culture of late night TV, dining and entertainment.

In the day modern work routines tend to undermine our eating the largest meal at midday which MAV recommends. Pitta people have strong digestions which require fuel. If they miss lunch-time they can become quite irritable.

Kapha types are naturally steadier but need longer sleep than others. They also need more exercise. Their rhythms are less easily disturbed but they will take longer to return to balance. Typically a Vata type will take more frequent short periods off work with quick recoveries from minor illnesses whether mental or physical. Pitta types have the ability to force them-selves to work even when not feeling great and Kapha types are slower to notice that stress, imbalance or depression is building up. They may take longer to recover when imbalance or fatigue accumulate and tip them over.

If daily routine is a problem in Western culture, our seasonal routines are even worse and our life-cycle appreciation very poor. Our dominant urban culture has separated us from most seasonal influences. If you drive from the underground car-park of your apartment building to the same in your office block each day, you may need to consult the internet to remember what season it is. The ready availability of food from far away or frozen long ago, allows us freedom to eat anything at any time of year. This is a sort of freedom but one that forgets that our bodies evolved rather closer to the natural environment including the seasons. Favouring food which balances the seasonal effects on our physiology is a powerful preventative strategy.

One of the most dramatic changes in human life over the last century has been to our life-cycle. This has become much longer and is still increasing. 60 is the new 40 and no-one is quite sure what 90 or 100 are all about. Old age used to be a short period before death but the number of people over 65 or over 85 is increasing rapidly and we need to find good roles for our advanced years. Perhaps the focus on nuclear families will need rethinking so older people have more function as grand-parents. More radical is the recognition of our later years as a spiritual and inward time. For the elderly, depression is common and is harder to treat being more likely to become persistent. This can be seen in biological terms of the body having less recovery power. It can also be seen in relation to the elderly having no useful role. Many are also without much spiritual faith or understanding. As Jung pointed out, depression in old age often has to do with facing death and mortality and we are poorly equipped to answer the important questions here.

At the other end of adult-hood adolescence has grown from being a few embarrassing years to a couple of decades. Unstable routines, relationships, and self-image, and excess alcohol use have become the norm for a long period of many lives. These are potent risks for mood disorders. Partly this reflects economic change with young people being able to leave home, partly geographical mobility, and partly changes in contraception and pregnancy planning. Another driver is the lack of a strong and convincing Adult culture to compete with the more transient attractions of Youth culture. Not enough adults are sufficiently mature in terms of their moral and spiritual development. Role models are not seen often enough to inspire young people to grow up. If you do not fully develop psychologically then you risk finding adult life, when family responsibility and stability finally arrive, as unsatisfying and depressing.

Physical health

The reduced life expectancy for people with long term mental illness is in large part due not to suicide but to heart disease. MAV interventions have been shown to reduce many of the cardio-vascular risk factors with reduction of stress, blood pressure, cholesterol levels, and smoking. Some MAV food supplements show very high anti-oxidant activity. At the more positive end of physical health we see an emphasis in sports on the mental fitness of athletes. They are obsessional about their diets and exercise routines but also about their mental focus and stress levels. They know the value of fine tuning their minds as well as their bodies.

It is unfortunate that Psychiatry has evolved into such a separate discipline from the physical braches of medicine. Even Neurology is quite distant. Recently there has been increased interest in the relationship of physical and mental health. People with mental problems are found to have high co-morbidities of physical illness and shorter lives. As already discussed the common problems of mental depression and physical heart disease have very close links and shared causes. Amazingly we have only recently recognised or rediscovered the value of physical exercise in mental health, especially for depression.

The separation of Psychiatry and general medicine is one reason why the basics of physical health such as diet have been largely ignored in psychiatry. MAV sees much less difference between the mind and the body. Western science is catching up with discoveries such as the immense number of neuro-transmitters and receptors found outside the nervous system. Even on the level of biochemistry and cellular functions the body now seems much more intelligent than we thought. The World Health Organisation says there is no health without mental health. It is equally true that there is little chance of real mental health without good physical health.

Jennifer

Jennifer was a 28 year old lady, sadly already divorced, who worked in a bank. She had some family history of depression but had not been depressed herself previously. Her life had become perhaps too busy since her marriage ended with much social life and not quite enough sleep and she was exercising less. She had found in her teens that she felt better when physically active but had let this go in the last year or two. She had a positive and steady personality, was much valued at work and was somebody others often relied on.

She had drifted into a depressed state over a few months during the winter. She had considered whether she had a seasonal problem but could not remember being this down in the winter before. Friends had tried to boost her up by including her in more social events and these were often in the evenings. She did not drink much alcohol and had never been tempted by more exotic drugs.

Jennifer was predominantly Kapha in her constitution. She was steady and strong, learned slowly but then retained learning well. She disliked cold weather and could not wake up for work without an alarm clock. Kapha types need more hours of sleep and this meant she needed to go to bed earlier and resist too many late night events. As Kapha digestion is also slower she was advised to not much later in the evening as this would disturb her sleeping.

She had discovered for herself that she benefited from exercise and when fit had good stamina. The best time to exercise for her was between 6 and 10 either AM or PM which are the Kapha influenced times of day. She was persuaded to join a morning running group and went on to run a half-marathon the next year. She reported that she pounded some of her angry thoughts about her ex-husband into her running.

Jennifer had some good assets including her friends and her own determination to change for the better. She found the advice of MAV guided her efforts to become much more successful in increasing her mood and energy level. She later learned TM and achieved more results especially regarding mental energy and hope for the future.

Five Senses

Our five main senses relate to the five elements in MAV: earth, water, fire, air, and *akasha* (which translates to space or space-time). These are subtle concepts. Kapha for example is composed of earth and water and so relates to the structure and fluids of the body both at a superficial level in terms of Kapha types being physically large and strong and at the microscopic cellular level. The five senses: smell, taste, sight, touch, and hearing correspond to the five elements. They reflect fundamental ways in which consciousness is active, five ways in which our intelligence is aware of the intelligence in the body and environment.

Hearing

In Ayurveda hearing is the most subtle sense relating to *akasha*. At their finest level the laws of nature are vibrations and when directly experienced by an enlightened person they are heard in consciousness as the Vedas. The Vedic sounds can be chanted aloud or even written down but their power is at the deeper levels. Using sounds in your own mind can remind the physiology of its ideal blueprint – formed by the laws of nature. Vibration can also be gently applied by a trained practitioner in MAV.

At a more superficial level there is still some merit to listening to Vedic recitation and EEG studies show very calm and coherent brainwaves in people so listening. There is also a whole branch of Vedic Science devoted to music, Ghandarva Veda. This emphasises the effect of music on maintaining balance to the natural rhythms of life. Specific pieces relate to different times of day or season. Most of us have certain music we play when we need calming down or energising. Ghandarva Veda has some effective options for different times and situations. The breakdown of biological rhythms is a strong risk for imbalance in the body.

The natural environment is just as much an expression of the laws of nature as we are and listening to natural sounds will be more harmonious than artificial mechanical noise. This has become important in urban life where there is a constant background of electronic and machine activity.

An easier way than time travel to leave the stress of modern life behind is through meditation, considered in the next chapter. Transcendental Meditation uses a natural process of refining the sound value of thought to reach a level of inner silence within us.

Ironically it is silence that provides the most blissful therapy in the sense of hearing.

Touch

Massage is a part of the best daily routine according to MAV. Oil massage has various effects. Pressure on the skin, muscles and tissues benefits the circulation. Oil is absorbed and aids the purification process. Unless you are extremely wealthy or have a most generous partner a regular morning massage is likely to be done by yourself. This has an advantage as when you touch each area of the body your attention goes there and your sense of touch gives a feedback loop to your brain and consciousness. Putting attention on parts of the body that need rebalancing is useful.

Purification can be achieved through a process called Panchakarma, ideally at every change of season. One of the central ingredients of Panchakarma is whole body massage performed by trained masseurs. Along with steam baths and digestive purification this drives impurities through and out of the body.

MAV uses a specific form of touch in its Pulse Diagnosis. A trained expert can use this to diagnose both your underlying constitution and your current imbalances. The qualities of Vata, Pitta, and Kapha can be felt in the pulse and with experience also their sub-divisions and the layers of the different tissues in the physiology. This is very strange to a Western-trained physician and it depends on the MAV understanding of how the body is an expression of the laws of nature. In Western medicine we only see these laws as expressed through biochemistry building up the substance and functioning of the body. In MAV we see these laws as being expressed through layers of intelligence within consciousness and being experienced through the senses. It is even more useful to take your own pulse regularly. You become familiar with its changes through the day, after digestion, through the month and seasonal cycles and can detect imbalances early on. When we are depressed we lose touch with our body ignoring its needs. Regular use of massage and Pulse taking will counteract this.

One of the best known parts of the Vedic Tradition is Yoga, already mentioned in the last chapter. Again Yoga can be seen on the one hand to stretch and physically stimulate parts of the body and on the other to point our conscious attention to parts of the body stimulating their intelligence level.

Touch relates to the element of air and breathing exercises are a part of Yoga commonly used both to calm the nerves and to invigorate the body. Breathing in MAV is related to the more subtle energy levels and rhythms in the body. Neurophysiology studies do demonstrate that breathing relates to the activity of the autonomic nervous system and hormonal rhythms.

Sight

This sense is less used in MAV at a gross level though there is advice on which colours affect which constitutions. As with sound, natural environments are held to have a positive effect on mood and there is some emerging evidence. We all experience the differing effects of concrete urban surroundings to a green natural place. Being outside is also good for making sure you get enough sunlight, known to be good for Seasonal Affective Disorder and Vitamin D production.

Light does have its own subtle levels and there is an MAV therapy called Maharishi Light Therapy with Gems. This applies light through gemstones to specific points on the body. One explanation of why gemstones are so valued is that the light they produce has refined positive healing effects.

Taste

Diet is a huge part of MAV covering what to eat, when to eat it and how to eat. The self-referral aspect is simply becoming more aware of what you like and what is good for you. Habit is a big part of food choice, both our individual habits and those of our family and culture. Western diets have become unbalanced from an MAV perspective. The excess of sweet, sour, and salty tastes do act to counter-balance our Vata excess but they also give us the metabolic problems of obesity and diabetes. Anxious depression related to Vata is often associated with eating too much and putting on weight. Experience and knowledge of the other main tastes, pungent, bitter, and astringent, have been diminished. Using all six tastes is more satisfying and more fulfilling so we have less desire to over-eat.

MAV has a wide knowledge of herbal medicines and they are analysed for their intelligence value using the same qualities that we use to understand food. MAV holds that if your diet is well balanced then this will be more powerful than medicines. The emphasis is on prevention. The poor diets of depressed people are often thought to be secondary to their being depressed. More likely there is a vicious circle of poor mood and poor diet worsening each other as we become less conscious of what is good for us.

Chemistry is a complex level of life as there are thousands of different chemicals in every cell. This complexity has stopped us finding ideal drugs or magic bullets. It also makes it tough to intellectually analyse the chemical effects of our diet. We cannot calculate all of these even with a computer let alone in our daily life but all these biological chemicals are expressions of DNA and ultimately expressions of the Unified Field of the laws of nature. We could live in accordance with the laws of nature by having this unified level of intelligence lively in our awareness. Intellectually we struggle to comprehend all the chemicals and the many laws of nature active at one time. But the essence of nature and of natural law is that these strands of intelligence are unified. The separation of natural law is only an intellectual conceit. MAV teaches that we can appreciate the wholeness of a balanced state of health and our senses like taste can guide us to retain that balance without excessive intellectual analysis.

Knowing when to eat is basic to our diet and health. Ideally we eat enough to satisfy our hunger but not too much. If balanced we are hungry again at the time of our next meal-time. Over-eating leads to obesity of course but also to poorly digested food and incomplete metabolism leading to build up of harmful impurities in the system. Learning to eat only when hungry is a simple technique to learn.

Smell

Smell is a strong and primitive sense and in MAV is said to be the least subtle relating to the earth element. Aroma therapy is a part of MAV again aimed at balancing the Doshas or qualities in your physiology. Aromas can be used for relaxation and aiding sleep, which is the most common use but also for enervating and stimulating the body.

Non-toxic building materials are advised by MAV to reduce harmful chemicals in the living environment. Even if we are not consciously aware of each chemical we do notice the effect of living or working in buildings that are either pure or polluted. Whether outgassing toxic materials could play a major place in the frequency of modern depression is not clear.

Time

MAV is very concerned with the daily, monthly and seasonal rhythms in our physiology and mirrored in our environment. Vedic knowledge also covers the longer cycles of time through our lifespan. To Western science it remains a most annoying mystery as to why episodes of depression occur when they do. Sometimes there are obvious life events or behavioral changes but often these are not enough to explain the severity of illness. Vedic science finds that there are longer term cycles but these are complicated. The science of Jyotish is dedicated to their study.

On a simpler level the influence of the three Doshas changes through life in their usual sequence of Kapha, Pitta, and Vata. This is one reason why anxiety and depression become common in old age with Vata becoming stronger. Older adults are less tolerant of change and more comfortable with routine. They need less sleep and are less active but can still be very inspirational to others. The big question about time in the life-cycle is how long do we live. The baby boomer generation is pumping research money into this question. Having good mental health is certainly a main ingredient to a long life as well as a happy one. Too many people are not finding the last chapters in their life fulfilling ones. MAV has a whole section on length of life called Rasayana. This emphasises the basics of MAV such as diet, routine, life-supporting activity and meditation. It specifically identifies some herbal preparations for improving the immune system. Amrit Kalash has a definite claim to being the oldest such preparation and its use is being validated by modern science for example in its anti-oxidant activity. Research shows an improvement in stress related symptoms as well as improvements in immune function.

MAV and the Self

MAV describes the self as the deepest part of the mind, the basis of all our experience. We have a small self which comprises our individuality and a large Self which is just pure consciousness. This is the goal of meditation. It provides a field of peace and energy beyond the level of our stresses and negative thoughts. This state of mind is paralleled by coherence in the brainwaves and this same pattern is seen in many of the other aspects of MAV which use the various senses.

If we can achieve a cleaner and more natural state of body and nervous system then we become more able to experience this deepest state of mind. We also become more aware of what is good for us. Ultimately we can use our senses to guide us more than intellectual knowledge. This can be seen as our senses growing clearer and more accurate or we can say that our consciousness has within it the laws of nature and we spontaneously become more in tune with them and so live more healthy lives. The research on addiction illustrates this. Most addiction therapies are focussed directly on the addiction but have disappointingly low success rates. People who learn TM for any reason tend to spontaneously use less addictive substances, legal and illegal and this effect is cumulative over time. As the body becomes purer it naturally craves less harmful drugs.

MAV uses the field of consciousness because it holds this to be the basis of our subjective experience and our material body. If this is so then we would expect to find the laws of intelligence expressing themselves in similar ways. The Vedas and Vedic expressions are said by MAV to be direct expressions of the laws of nature. The unique feature of the human brain is that it can when enlightened experience these laws subjectively. This concept led to the recent description by neuro-scientist Dr Nader of how the structure of the brain parallels the structure of all the various areas of Vedic knowledge. This shows the brain is an expression of natural law not just in vague terms of obeying the laws of chemistry and physics, but in our brain's structure being a detailed representation of natural law. This opens the way to using particular parts of the Veda to balance individual parts of the brain, a most exciting area of research.

Richard and MAV

How would Richard's visit been different if the natural health practitioner in the last chapter had been MAV trained? There would have been a clear directive to learn meditation for its own benefits to mood and as an under-pinning to other modes of therapy. As a teacher himself Richard would appreciate the value of learning new skills and it would suit him to do something to help himself.

Secondly there would have been similar but stronger advice on daily routine as a building block of health. Regarding diet, there would be emphasis on eating more midday and not skipping lunch and not eating too late in the evening. As Richard was not up to complex cookery he could consider using simple herb and spice seasoning to add to his food to help balance his Doshas. The specialist would have taken Richard's pulse to determine which Doshas were most out of balance. A first consultation would be too soon to look at self-pulse diagnosis but Richard could be given literature as to the future possibilities.

As Richard's life was spaced by school terms he could consider putting more time into his health in the holidays. This could include daily oil massage, which again might be too big an ask initially, or he could go for a course of Panchakarma to shift more fatigue and stress.

A good selling point for MAV is that some of the basic advice is the most powerful. The benefits of learning meditation are usually rapid with students feeling brighter, less stressed, and having better sleep and more energy. As time passes and the mind and body grow clearer Richard would find himself making healthier choices, like drinking less alcohol, more easily. When his nervous system is less stressed he needs fewer artificial props.

Richard was quite focussed on his feelings of stress and depression, and MAV changes should help these. However they would also aid other areas of his life and hopefully raise his sights as to what he could achieve. An MAV specialist would not tell him what to do with his life, but if his mind and body start functioning better he can turn his attention from just surviving each day to the longer term goals of life.

Knower, Knowing and Known in MAV

If you visit a specialist in MAV it is possible to remain in the role of the object of knowledge and let him or her make an assessment and give advice. However they will want to engage you in the process of knowing by asking for your observations about yourself. They will also encourage you to become more of an observer of your behavior and life-style. If you proceed to learn pulse diagnosis the self-referral loop grows stronger and you close the circle between Knower, Knowing and Known.

MAV is a source of intellectual knowledge which you can own as well as being a method by which your subjective awareness of your health strengthens. Underlying both is the field of consciousness. Familiarity with consciousness in its most settled state enables faster learning and supports more spontaneous healthy choices.

The deeper wisdom of Vedic science is that the apparent separation of Knower, Knowing and Known is only dominant when our mind is imbalanced or immature. When the mind's full potential is reached, which should be the normal state of mental health; it is the unity of Knower, Knowing and Known that prevails. The neurotic negative inner commentary of the small self in our mind becomes quiet.

Effectiveness of MAV in Depression

The strongest evidence comes from research on TM which is in the next chapter. While Ayur Veda is several millennia old, MAV has only recently been re-established or re-discovered as it brings back the most fundamental knowledge of the Vedic tradition.

There is growing evidence in physical health and mental well-being. Perhaps most important is that the mood of average people who do not think of themselves as at all depressed improves. Mood fluctuations are less. Sleep is improved which is crucial for reducing the risk of depression.

People following MAV tend to use several parts such as TM, daily routine, diet, food supplements and Panchakarma. This makes the study of individual aspects harder. Interestingly the physiological research on brain functioning shows similar increased coherence patterns in a variety of different MAV treatments. This is thought to be a marker for improving our level of consciousness and maturity of the nervous system.

Which people are comfortable with MAV?

MAV has a number of different approaches within it and everyone should be able to find something that appeals. As with Natural Medicine generally there is a spectrum from specialist advice to self-help and education. A unique aspect of MAV is the use of consciousness as the basis of all health. For this reason learning meditation is a central recommendation. It is possible to benefit from MAV without learning meditation but the profit will be less.

MAV can certainly be approached in stages with a small amount of advice going a long way. If you already have a generally good diet and daily routine, MAV adds knowledge of your individual constitution to fine tune this.

MAV has its value in treatment but it is ideally used for prevention and maintaining a higher level of health and mood than is usually aimed for. This is attractive if you are in good health or if you have been depressed in the past and are keen to avoid relapses. If you are responsible for other people including children then MAV has much to offer to help you promote their health.

MAV is not a form of counselling and does not explore past emotional problems. It supports a journey to self-knowledge in terms of knowing one's constitution and also in terms of the deepest experience of our own self-awareness but it is not caught up in the knots of past conflicts and relationships.

Summary

MAV is a recent rediscovery of Ayur Veda with the role of consciousness being remembered as the basis to mental and physical health. It uses techniques of consciousness such as TM and its other methods emphasise finer levels of intelligence and self-referral. Knowledge of your constitutional type allows you to be more aware of influences from diet, activity and daily routine that support or stress your state of balance. Even the subtle art of pulse diagnosis is ideally learned by a patient to close the self-referral loop not just used by an expert.

MAV encompasses therapies using all five senses and places great emphasis on natural rhythms but all of these reflect qualities of consciousness. Pure consciousness has qualities of integration, stability, balance and fortunately of bliss. As for natural approaches in general MAV seeks to purify the body and raise it to higher levels of health and resistance to aging and illness.

Key Points from MAV

∞ Consciousness is the basis of the mind and the body and the environment

∞ Each person has a constitution that is a balance of three Doshas, aspects of natural law

∞ Knowing your-self and having clearer senses allow a spontaneously healthier life

∞ A healthier and longer life should be our normal expectation.

Challenge for MAV

Ayur Vedic medicine is still being re-established following its period of suppression in the colonial era and has been recognised by the WHO as an important medical tradition. Maharishi Ayur Veda is a great leap forward as part of a re-integration of Vedic knowledge. Its challenge is to educate the public to accept that consciousness is a fundamental part of mental and physical health. Western psychological traditions have been very concerned with emotions and then with cognitive processes and have not given enough attention to the field of consciousness in which all these experiences occur.

Another challenge is to persuade us to spend more time and effort on maintaining health rather than just treating disease after it occurs. This should be an obvious strategy for depression which is so often a recurrent problem.

∞ Chapter 9 ∞
Discovering Inner Bliss
Transcendental Meditation

Meditation is growing in popularity and like Natural Medicine it comes in many forms. Some methods use concentration or focus on a sensory experience such as staring at a candle. Some prefer contemplation of a desirable idea or quality like compassion. Mindfulness comprises a mixture of focus on present sensation and experience with acceptance of or detachment from judgmental and negative thoughts. Meditations can be simple or more like a computer game of going through different topics and levels. Religious traditions have their meditations often using contemplation while at the secular end basic relaxation exercises use breathing or muscle relaxation techniques which activate the mind's relaxation response allowing the body to rest.

Meditation may have a specific goal such as improving mental focus or a religious ideal. In contrast to relaxation meditation commonly seeks to put the mind in a different state of awareness which is not just restfulness but is more settled than the usual waking state. To do this we need to get through the surface layer of external sensation and the chatter of our ever-flowing superficial thoughts. There are a number of ways of doing this some of which are counter-intuitive. Focusing on an outer sensation can distract us from other sensory channels and when we get bored rigid with the single focus our minds may move inwards. There are a number of hypnotic tricks such as concentrating on a meaningless phrase such as "more is less" which freezes the intellect and may allow the mind to sneak past it to more intuitive realms. Zen Buddhism is famous for challenging the intellect and it is from here that the recent schools of mindfulness come.

The Vedic tradition has given us Transcendental Meditation (TM) which as the name suggests has the goal of Transcending not just beyond the surface of the mind but beyond all relative or individual thoughts. This meditation was widely taught by Maharishi Mahesh Yogi who also rejuvenated Ayur Veda. He recognized that in the West meditation had a reputation for being a reclusive practice, hard to do and not related success in the material world. He emphasized that meditation was easy, was suitable for everyone not just strange men in the Himalayas, and encouraged research into its benefits. TM is the most widely researched form of meditation and has been increasingly taken up by a wide array of people from businessmen and sportsmen to students who want to succeed in their very practical and physical spheres of life. The benefits come from spending 20 minutes twice a day allowing the mind to transcend. A striking finding is that the average mood of TM practitioners increases. Improved mood, confidence and energy support increased well-being. TM can be seen as a mental bath to improve our psychological hygiene or a mental fitness program.

At the basis of the mind is a field of Pure Consciousness in which we are just aware of being aware. A key area of research has been physiological showing that with the subjective experience of Pure Consciousness the body is also in a new state of restful alertness. This is different to the simple rest that we enjoy from relaxation exercises. The EEG during TM shows high levels of coherence across the brain. This coherence spreads much more widely than we see in mindfulness and the progress over time is also much faster. This correlates with the historical findings from the Zen tradition that it is not easy to progress beyond the basic benefits of mindfulness to full enlightenment of the mind.

TM uses a natural ability of the mind to move to more enjoyable experiences. Deeper and more settled levels of attention are both more relaxed and more alert. The experience of Pure Consciousness combines silence and dynamism, an attractive combination which allows us to recharge our batteries. The secret to TM is that it is effortless with no concentration or straining. It uses thoughts which have sound value but no intellectual meaning which might distract us.

These sounds known as mantras are suitable for the individuals learning and the technique needs to be taught in person not from a book. The success of TM comes from it being a simple effortless technique using the nature of the mind to go towards the pleasant and expanded experience of its own deeper levels.

Why does it then need to be taught? People who learn do find the experience of transcending is a natural experience, not strange, and many feel it is like a memory of something they knew was there in their mind's potential. But just as language is a natural ability which needs to be learned we do need to be instructed in how to transcend. From our own experience we may transcend in other circumstances such as when moved by a work of art, or love, or having a peak experience in sport. TM just provides a reliable regular method of letting the mind dive within, a daily mental bath, or mental refreshment.

Finding inner calm

Mary was a 32 year old lady who worked in sales. When she was on form she could sell anything as she was very smart and very attractive. Unfortunately her mood was quite unstable with both long swings of several months which were mild and short lived severe changes. She could go from happy to suicidal in a day. She had been diagnosed with possible Bipolar Disorder but medication for this did not help much and her faster mood swings remained her main worry. She had never really been manic and when in a good mood she was very functional. In depressed mood her self-confidence would plummet and her anxiety levels would go through the roof.

Mary had good insight and also the sense to keep contact with her long-suffering boy-friend who was very supportive and stable. She could not live with him as she would often get too irritable to be around but he remained one of her few anchors in the stormy seas of her moods. She also kept very fit with running and aerobics. She had flirted with addictions and become quite unwell with stimulant drugs a couple of times but managed to escape from that trap in her late twenties. Psychotherapy was of limited help. She knew all the cognitive strategies but they would not stop moods changing and she had no obvious history of abuse or neglect to deal with.

She was not one to sit down and relax either being too busy enjoying life or too down to care. She did have bit of a mentor or coach at her gym and on his advice tried TM as a mental partner to her physical exercise program.

She found almost immediately deep periods of inner calm in her meditation and was surprised to find this inside her as previously she had rarely been happy when not active. On this basis she was able to slow down a bit when happy and her anxiety level when down was much improved. She also found her confidence was better. She had always been confident of her ability to impress and persuade others when in a good frame of mind but to this was added a self confidence that was independent of others' opinions.

There is some evidence that any type of relaxation and probably most meditations will help to some degree with stress and may improve your mood. The evidence with TM is that all aspects of mental and physical health are improved. As the practice expands our mind to become more conscious, the use of TM can be seen from the perspectives of all the different approaches we have considered in earlier chapters. Consciousness is the field in which all other experiences occur so strengthening our very consciousness should be expected to help our thoughts, feelings, and behavior.

TM and Behavioral Therapy

Practicing TM twice a day is in itself a pleasant activity. It also improves the enjoyment we gain from activity outside of meditation. The restful alertness of the TM experience is a great antidote to a stressful busy life where our minds are full of thoughts but not enough seems to be accomplished. The practice of meditation is entirely internal and so is not dependent on the changing circumstances of our lives. Meditation gives a reliable regular experience of peace of mind. This balances the active side of life, as sleep does. TM allows a deeper type of rest which we enjoy because we remain conscious. TM also improves the quality of our sleep and improves insomnia.

Behavior theory sees our actions as being goal directed, to gain reward and we usually think of external rewards as being sensory, financial, material or romantic. Emotional rewards are more complex as they are experienced internally but usually involve other people, who are external. The experience of Pure Consciousness is totally internal but is very rewarding. TM is easy just because the deeper levels of the mind are more pleasant and the most blissful is the underlying field of consciousness in its pure state. We can also say this is the most settled state of the mind with awareness but no specific thought. The attention naturally goes for this if given the chance. Pure Consciousness is also the closest reward as it is our own Self.

Another reason that TM is easy is that you just have to do it. You do not have to understand the mechanism intellectually or even believe it will work. Like the best behavioral strategies it simply requires repetitive practice. As the mind becomes more familiar with its subtler levels the qualities of these levels such as restfulness and intelligence become suffused into our normal waking state. It is nice to have some understanding but this is not a prerequisite and TM can be learned by people of any level of intelligence. This is true of Behavior Therapy in general. Learning is the basis of Behavior Therapy and we learn through doing.

One of the most difficult aspects of depression is the reduction in pleasure we feel even when engaged in activity that we would normally love. This is damage to the reward pathway itself. It reduces our drive and energy and makes life look grey. The clarity of mind that results from TM leads to strengthening of the reward mechanism so we enjoy ourselves more. This is why people learning TM find their activity level increasing. They do not become recluses.

TM and Cognitive Therapy

The first step in Cognitive Therapy is to step back from the superficial level of thinking and observe your thoughts. This is a relative level of transcending. TM takes this path to its conclusion in that level of the mind which is beyond all thinking. Cognitive Therapy uses a process of observing and analyzing thoughts. This is useful but has its limits as we can only go to a certain level of abstraction intellectually. TM uses the natural ability of the mind to transcend without analytic processing. The intellect remains awake if only to discriminate different levels of awareness but it is not engaged to analyze or criticize our performance. A theoretical understanding of how the mind develops and of higher states of consciousness is available in the Vedic tradition but this is not primary.

The expansion of the mind through TM gives many of the results of Cognitive Therapy in terms of improved problem solving, more independence of mind or self-directedness, and of course improved mood. This is true for people who previously believed their mood was normal or OK not just people who felt low. One of the novel benefits of TM is that the basic intelligence level improves and this is reflected in students' results. Our core abilities such as attention and memory are refined as the mind becomes less stressed. This is also useful after a depression as our cognitive abilities such as concentration and memory are often slow to recover.

As we spend more time in the deeper realms of our mind through daily practice we strengthen the more profound aspects of mental life. These include our values, moral reasoning, spiritual beliefs as well as our family and work relationships. We saw in Acceptance and Commitment Therapy that aligning your action with your values was important. Having more awareness of these deeper values allows us to do this spontaneously.

TM is essentially a mental process. In the practice of TM what we do is think and allow our thinking to become less and less and yet remain awake. TM is a pure form of Cognitive Therapy. It establishes the basic field of consciousness in the mind. Once this is stable we can go on to promote thoughts from this deepest level of the mind and this is taught in the more advanced TM Sidhi Program.

TM and Psychoanalysis

Psychoanalysis is all about self-knowledge and discovering or uncovering the unconscious areas of the mind. Freud recognised that the Ego or small self is only one part of the internal world. He struggled to find the larger Self and saw life as an uneasy alliance or compromise between our higher functions and lower appetites. His methods took a long time and were not always successful. Integration of unconscious material and gaining of insight was difficult. As with Cognitive Therapy analysing all the layers of the mind in order to expand our awareness has its limitations. There are many emotional blocks and the ultimate goal is not very clear.

More recent schools have been more positive and some have acknowledged the transcendent though not usually as the basic field in which all other experience occurs. This idea is very close to field theories in modern physics however.

Freud detailed the relationships between the states of consciousness of waking and dreaming. He described their different languages and logic. He was less concerned with the sleep state as there is so little apparent mental activity and he did not like the transcendental state much. Although he was all for understanding the inner workings of the mind he saw too much inward attention as unhealthy and narcissistic. He invented various ways of encouraging his patients to let their unconscious speak but he did not have a simple method to let them transcend. Nor did he spend time analysing the psychologies of enlightened people. His ideas about mental health derived from the study of ill, mainly neurotic, people. He saw health as the absence of conflicts and blocks or excessive anxiety rather than being a very positive state.

The Vedic tradition sees waking, dreaming and sleeping as the three relative changing states and Transcendental or Pure Consciousness as the underlying non-changing state. What changes is our ability to experience it. Pure Consciousness is not just another thought, feeling or experience to be had but the basis of all experience. This is the key ingredient missing from Psychoanalysis because our large Self is that field of Pure Consciousness. It is beyond analysis as only it can fully experience itself.

As we saw in comparison to Cognitive Therapy, TM goes for expanding the mind first rather than intellectual, or in the case of analysis emotional, understanding. How does TM get rid of stresses and blocks in the mind without re-experiencing them? There are several mechanisms according to Vedic Science. Firstly these mental stresses have their physical parallels in the brain. The deep rest of TM allows these stresses to be released or normalised without having to re-experience or understand their original historical cause. Secondly when consciousness becomes brighter and knowledge increases then the darkness of ignorance vanishes. The classic example is that your fear of seeing a snake disappears when you realise what you saw was an illusion and just a snake-shaped piece of string. A third process involves the growth of higher mental abilities. As a child grows its mental ability and capacity to understand the world grows. This should continue much further than it does for most adults. The qualities of post-operational growth (beyond Piaget's normal levels of cognitive development) are described in modern psychology and include being able to entertain more than one paradigm at once, to tolerate differences, and to appreciate the spiritual dimension of life. Such progress allows us to better understand or move on from many emotional problems.

Relationships are vital in Psychoanalysis and are the topic of endless discussion, some useful and some just psycho-babble, in the modern era. Individuals who are less stressed and in better mood, who have higher understanding, do enjoy better relationships and there is evidence for this with TM practitioners both at work and home. Besides these superficial reasons there is the role of Pure Consciousness. This field is experienced by us as individuals but it is a field that underlies all of us. Again this is parallel to the field theories in physics where individual particles such as electrons as seen as expressions of a single underlying electron field. We are so enamoured of ourselves as individuals we have forgotten our underlying connectedness. Perhaps this is why romantic love is such an obsession in present times. Love is a powerful feeling of connection so intense that the other is as important and as close as one-self. Leaving aside the sexual and emotional aspects there is a longing for unity with another person. The establishment of the transcendental level of consciousness in meditation is the basis on which our external or relative life can grow so we appreciate that other people and the world in general are part of the same field of consciousness.

Psychoanalysis puts a burden on its patients by telling them the external world is a reflection of their internal world. This internal world in turn can be seen as being structured by your early parenting and relationships. There is little point in looking for other people in the present to blame for your depression and it is probably too late to blame your parents. The positive side of this message is that you have the ability to change yourself. The negative side is that the world is imperfect and our ability to deal with it is not all-encompassing so depression may be a realistic reaction. The Vedic view is far more optimistic. It agrees that the world is as you are but is much more hopeful that you can be happy. One aspect of enlightenment is not just seeing the glass half full but maintaining an inner bliss even in circumstances that others find oppressive.

Psychoanalysis was responsible for the idea that personality was fixed from a young age and was very hard to change which is bad news if you have a personality disorder. A major psychological advance in recent decades has been to challenge this pessimism. The potential for our personality to grow is now much more accepted in modern therapy. Cloninger's description of personality consists of temperament and character. Temperament relates more to our fixed constitution strongly tied to our physiology. This has clear links to the tradition of the basic elements or principles or humours. Character is changeable with experience and more able to grow through maturity.

The three aspects or levels of character are Self-directedness, Cooperativeness, and Self-transcendence. The first relates to self-sufficiency and the second to our ability to relate to other people in a way that supports both them and our-selves. Self-directedness is low in most personality disorders and without this basis Cooperativeness also is less secure. The recognition of transcendence is an important step for modern psychology. This speaks to our relationship not just to other people but to the wider cosmos. The normal development of the personality should include this level. Maturity does include spirituality. This understanding has been blocked in a materialist culture. Material success has not been associated with higher levels of mental health and may even have discouraged maturity. Even in industry there is now progress with more awareness in the leadership of large companies that wider values and goals, aside from those of a financial nature, are desirable.

TM and Group Therapy

TM is an individual practice though some steps of the teaching are done in a group. Most people notice that their meditation is deeper when practiced in a group and research shows more physiological change especially in EEG coherence in a group. Practical considerations mean that meditation is usually done on your own or with immediate family or work colleagues if they are meditators. The benefits are both to the individual and the wider group. There is considerable research on companies who have had their employees learn TM. Putting aside 20 minutes twice a day to close the eyes may not seem the best way to improve productivity but it does. Mistakes and time off for illness reduce and cooperation between workers increases. The same is seen in schools where staff and students use TM. The whole atmosphere of the place changes to become quieter but more dynamic. Changes in collective consciousness reflect the individuals' changes.

Group therapy uses the strength of the group to create a therapeutic environment. It can become a place of safety, nourishing and learning. Connecting with other people is a good strategy for avoiding or dealing with depression. This is true for our lives in general not just specific therapy groups. TM gives us more sensitivity to others as well as more energy in ourselves. These and other psychological changes lead to better relationships. The deeper reason for relationships improving is the experience of the underlying field of consciousness. This underpins individual relationships and groups. The peace and strength of schools or work-places where everyone does TM is quite tangible. We may be more familiar with settings where the atmosphere is fragmented, muddled or turbulent. Even though everyone goes into a school with some intention to learn or to teach so many schools are fraught with problems of misbehaviour and lack of focus in class. It almost comes as a surprise to find schools where harmony and positivity dominate.

There is a startling area of research into collective consciousness being affected by TM. When 1% of the population are doing TM positive trends are seen in crime, accidents, economics and politics. This does not occur because meditators are campaigning for change. It happens because the whole quality of consciousness in the area changes. With the more advanced TM Sidhi program sudden changes are seen when large numbers of practitioners arrive in an area for a conference or training course. The statistics are very strong but this is still hard to believe.

We are all aware of collective consciousness in that we feel the mood of a place or a group but we assume the individuals create this through superficial interaction. Our experience of consciousness is rather limited to our individuality. Cultures with an extended family or tribal tradition are less restricted, seeing the group as the basic unit of life not the individual. Spending time at deeper levels of our individual mind connects us to other people very profoundly because we go beyond the world of differences and complexity to simpler and unifying realms of life.

If Agent Blue is to do with lack of connectedness then a group approach that could be taken on a large scale would be TM. The research shows that fairly small numbers of people creating coherence can affect the whole population. This has parallels in physics where a small percentage of molecules acting in synchrony can change the quality of the whole, for example in magnetism.

Biological Psychiatry and TM

TM gives a good rest to the mind and this can be easily measured in the body. Heart rate, respiration rate, and stress hormones all lower. The stress mechanism in the physiology becomes more finely tuned with lower levels of the higher control neuro-hormones. Unfortunately the brain is too complex to be certain how TM affects the levels of individual neuro-transmitters though there is indirect evidence serotonin function is enhanced.

There are multiple benefits to the physical health including heart disease. As we have seen depression and heart disease often go together. TM is the only well-proven meditation for heart disease and is recognised as such by the American Heart Association. There are measurable effects on blood pressure and cholesterol and some studies showing improvements in blood vessel walls. Overall health care costs reduce even for people with initially higher than average costs.

Another of the unwelcome companions of mental depression is a shorter life, not all due to heart disease. The effects of mental illness on the body's defence and repair mechanisms are more widespread, probably related to stress hormones and inflammatory chemicals. One of the most encouraging avenues of TM research looks at the slowing and in some cases reversal of the aging process. Even for people learning when already in their 80's there are measurable effects.

Biological Psychiatry is strongest for the more severe types of depression. TM might not be enough on its own if you are already in very dire straits but its role in prevention is valuable. Hospitalisation rates for mental disorder are lower in meditators showing a role in preventing severe illness. There is also some evidence for Bipolar Disorder. Rhythms are seen as vital in MAV and TM strengthens the daily routine by anchoring the day with two periods of deep rest. The ability to relax more also improves sleep and recovery from sleep deprivation is faster.

The state of Transcendental or Pure Consciousness is a subjective experience and during this state the physiology is also in a different state from waking dreaming or sleeping. As TM is practiced regularly the qualities of Transcendental Consciousness become available in our waking state. This includes improved mood and stability of mood. From the perspective of Vedic Science this is not a trip to a strange place but more of a returning home to a state of normal health. One reason why research into depression struggles is that the "normal" population which we compare depressed subjects to is not so normal. Having more subjects who have true maturity and strong mental health will lead to better insight in to the abnormalities of depression.

Significant progress is being made in research with the advent of better brain scanning technology. This is becoming fine enough to see brain changes in response to psychological stresses. The brain changes in children who are abused at an early age are a striking tragic example. For a long time physical abnormality was thought of as more important or powerful than psychological changes. Now we have better detectors we are seeing that psychological processes can lead to physical changes in structure and function. TM fits well into this new era as there are multiple studies showing the practice leads to profound brain development.

TM and Natural Medicine

As we have seen TM is an integral part of MAV. The refining of the nervous system sharpens our senses which means we can better judge for ourselves what is good for us. Dulling of the senses occurs with aging and with stress and with disuse. The common decline in hearing higher pitched sounds and difficulties with near-point vision are seen to be slower in meditators showing preservation of sensory function. Our reliance on chemical science has inadvertently led to us losing our natural ability to directly detect the quality of food through taste and smell. This has reached a point where we do not trust our senses to tell us what is good for us.

How much a better diet would protect us from depression remains unproven but this is the claim of Natural Medicine. This may seem too simple but we used to think exercise was too simple and we now accept exercise as a significant treatment for depression. Routines as already mentioned are improved by TM. Rhythms help the body maintain a dynamic stability. They also link us with the outside environment. Natural Medicine is very concerned with harmony between body and nature. This can be seen in changing one's diet and routine with the seasons or the use of naturally occurring herbs rather than artificially composed chemicals. The transcendental element provided by TM is the contact with the basic field of consciousness because this contains not only the seeds of our own intelligence but also the laws of nature underlying the outer world. Cultivating this field gives us a more spontaneous synchrony with nature. Our intuition and desires become healthier. A striking example of this is the reduction in use of addictive substances which is the opposite of what happens in depression where use increases. When you are stressed and depressed you are more likely to resort to short term fixes which are harmful long term. The more enlightened you are the less you will be tempted.

Richard and TM

If Richard had not gone to an MAV specialist but a TM teacher he would have started with the meditation on its own. He might have later picked up other aspects of MAV but many people just do the TM and gain good results.

Richard's life is already quite busy with a full time teaching job. He might have found it easier to learn in the holidays but he was able to learn in term attending the initial steps of teaching in the evening or at the weekend. Fitting the two periods of meditation in seemed tricky. The second period was easy as he did the TM when he returned home. This gave him a good rest and he was more able to enjoy the evening and less prone to drinking alcohol. The stress of the school day overshadowed his home time less. The morning meditation meant he had to get up a bit earlier which seemed a counter-intuitive way of getting rest. However it led to him going to bed a bit earlier and as his sleep was also better he did find himself starting the day in brighter mood.

His girl-friend noticed more improvement in him than he did himself and was herself motivated to learn. He was more like himself at the weekends and more able to enjoy himself. At work his problems did not magically go away but he gradually regained his confidence and was more able to stand back and look at his situation. He felt closer to some colleagues and found more help from their advice and general support than he had previously appreciated. Within himself he felt more at home even though he also became more aware of things that needed to change. The role of being a student on the TM course had been a useful swop for him reminding him that he could still learn skills and grow.

Later his attention might turn to that troublesome class and whether TM might help the children as well as improve the environment in which he worked.

Knower Knowing and Known in TM

TM uses the process of thinking or knowing and chooses a mantra with no intellectual meaning. This very specific object of knowledge then refines until the meditator transcends. This means the Knower aspect of the mind also goes deeper and transcends. As the Knower, process of Knowing and Known all go deeper they

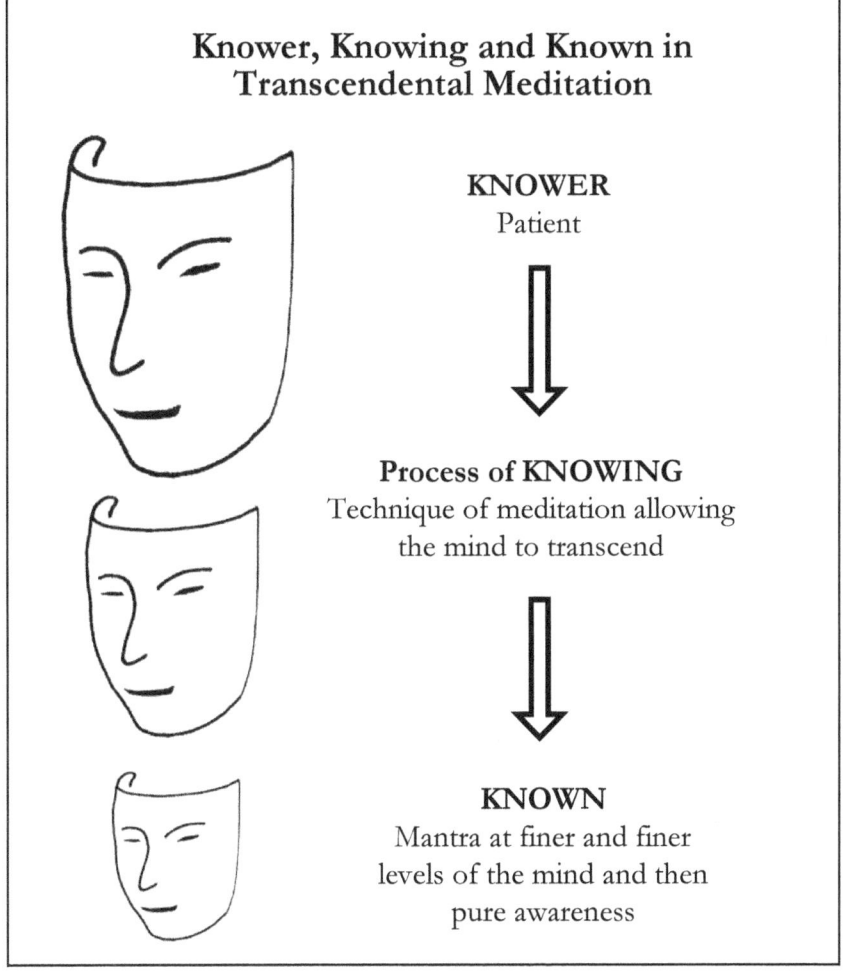

become closer and when relative thought is transcended they become one. This is the essence of consciousness that it is aware of itself, hence the name Pure Consciousness.

We experience the mantra or sound learned in TM at refined levels and we appreciate that our mind seems more settled but also larger. The Knower aspect from where we view experience or think thoughts is expanded. This is very welcome as we feel less restricted or bound by individual ideas, feelings or sensory inputs.

Learning TM does require a teacher but the teaching is delicate and puts the student straight into the position of Knower with experience of meditation leading any supporting knowledge. We have been used to being caught up in our senses and external relationships. Our small self is very defined by our roles and external qualities not to mention our physical bodies and other peoples' view of us. TM provides the balance of inner experience and of the larger Self which is pure subjectivity.

This experience of an expanded and unbounded state of mind is natural and pleasant. The energy and creativity reverberate in an experience of bliss. One does not have to be a quantum physicist to reach this level of experience. TM allows the mind to travel in this direction which it does naturally, travelling in the direction of greater happiness. It is necessary to have experience of this level to fully understand it. Just as external observation in physics cannot objectively be made beneath the Planck Scale, the Unified Field of natural law cannot be observed from outside. It can only experience itself and our special gift as humans is being able to align our individual consciousness with this universal level. From this basis we feel coherence with all the laws of nature and at home with the wholeness of knowledge.

Where does the growth of consciousness take us? Developmental psychology looks at our growth through childhood and adolescence. The human brain has evolved to support the development of language and a complex social life. It also enables experience of Pure Consciousness and spiritual alignment but this capacity is much less realised. Only a minority enjoy higher states of consciousness that lie within our potential. Many people suffer mental problems characterised by a lack of stability and immaturity. Borderline personality disorder sufferers pray for inner peace and a reliable sense of self. The tragedy of addiction is that it disables the very higher functions of the brain that you need to plan and find meaning in life. Depression puts a brake on our growth. Mental illness impedes the expansion of consciousness and may be a result of lack of maturity and integration.

Evolutionary psychiatry traces the development over millennia of our psychology. As animals evolve they are able to satisfy basic drives and needs such as food and safety and then move on to higher tasks. Depression is often associated with the frustration or failure to satisfy our drives, being poor or lonely or not progressing in our career. Focussing on the specific problems has some use but we have not looked enough at our underlying lack of growth in consciousness. If a ten year old was still behaving like a 6 year old we would spot this but the scarcity of truly mature adults means we have not recognised the lack of maturity that is so prevalent not just in sufferers from depression but in the whole population. Enlightenment is not seen by Vedic Science as an unusual state but as normal maturity.

Effectiveness of TM in Depression

The best evidence for TM is that it improves the mood of people who learn. This finding relates to people who learn TM for any reason. Many do learn because they feel stressed or low in mood or have insomnia but others learn to study better or run faster or for personal development. Many students start with an average mood which improves once they learn. TM has not been greatly used as a stand-alone treatment for depression. This is partly because TM is taught generally in an educational rather than clinical setting. TM teachers are not therapists or psychiatrists.

There is significant clinical experience among doctors and therapists who have referred their patients to learn TM as well as from some people qualified as both TM teachers and clinicians. TM has a definite role in prevention as shown by large health insurance data studies. Clinically it is a very good additional strategy. As we have discussed in this chapter TM would support most types of therapy and may enhance their effect.

There is stronger evidence in anxiety states and addiction which commonly form part of a depressive illness. The finding is that benefits accumulate over time as would be predicted if TM is fostering better balance and maturity of the mind. Depression is a long term risk for many and most treatments for depression are short term. The existing prevention data for TM is encouraging. On the other side of the coin there is good positive evidence for meditators becoming stronger and happier with time, less stressed and more resilient.

Which people are comfortable with TM?

Anyone can do TM. It requires no life-style change or belief or personality style. As it uses a natural ability of the mind anyone who can think can do TM. Sitting with eyes closed does not come easily to young children and they do a modified practice till age 10. It does not require a reclusive attitude, far from it. It will appeal to people who want to develop themselves in general and achieve enlightenment but it also works for those who want to deal with a specific problem in their lives.

As TM is easy and effortless it can be practiced when you are depressed and it does not require the more complex knowledge of most psychological therapies. It does, like Behavior Therapy, require that you actually do it, so you need to put aside the time for regular practice. Some of the most surprising results come to people who practice with no expectation or belief but are learning because their partner is or their work colleagues or sports team-mates. Unlike most psychological therapies no commitment to the theory or understanding of the mechanics is needed. This suits results oriented practical people. Those who want to get mentally fit to complement their physical fitness will also find TM a good match.

Summary

TM is a simple natural technique which can be learned by anyone. This meditation allows the mind to go towards its source or basis in Pure Consciousness, a state of restful alertness. TM gives a deep rest which gives us the energy for more dynamic activity and so is not a reclusive meditation. TM is well researched in terms of the physiological changes during the practice with characteristic brain wave coherence distinguishing it from other meditations and mindfulness. The benefits outside of meditation to mind body and our social environment are also well evidenced. These results are consistent with the Vedic assertion that the normal state of mind and of mood are much higher than we usually settle for.

Key Points from TM

- ∞ The most settled state of mind is Pure Consciousness simply aware of itself
- ∞ The mind can easily experience this state
- ∞ One quality of Pure Consciousness is bliss

Challenge for TM

TM offers a very challenging message, that our mental potential including our mood can be much higher than is usually achieved. TM is already popular as a self-development and educational technique. It is being used more extensively in anxiety and post-traumatic states than in depression in terms of research. We have tended to think of anxiety and PTSD as being stress related but depression not so much. Depression has also been more captured by the biological pharmaceutical paradigm and Cognitive Therapy is a well proven psychological therapy already in the market. The place for TM may be more in prevention, adjunctive therapy and in the elevation of the whole population mood. Finding a way to improve mood and mental health for the population is an issue facing the world's health organisations today and TM is a good candidate. The focus of TM is on positive progress towards bliss and its challenge is to remind us that it has a role in combatting the major manifestation of mental stress in the world, depression.

∞ Chapter 10 ∞
Pathways from Depression to Bliss

We have seen that there are many factors in depression and many possible paths to recovery. A number of therapies are making progress in offering solutions though these do not always lead to complete health and happiness. There are positive movements to reduce the stigma of being mentally ill and there is more recognition of the importance of mental health. All in all this is a good time to expect more understanding and more action to deal with the global problem that depression has become.

The identification of so many causes leads to various interpretations. One is that depression is like heart disease where we acknowledge several important areas that all need attention. For the health of your heart you have to deal with smoking, cholesterol, diabetes, blood pressure, and stress levels. There is not a single simple cause of cardiac illness for most people. Another interpretation is that we have failed to find the deeper underlying factor. Agent Blue has been elusive to those searching for it. Another lesson from heart disease is that the average or currently "normal" mood in society may be low. Just as many people have a mildly or moderately high blood pressure or cholesterol which increases their risk of heart disease, there are many of us with less than optimal mood putting us at risk of depression severe enough to be seen as an illness. We need to raise our expectation of what is a normal mood.

There has been some growth of interest in the use of our natural strengths and more optimism in our ability to change and learn even as adults. We need to progress our paradigm of mental health to extend this optimism and set much loftier goals. Psychiatry has become too preoccupied with the fascinating details of pathology. Mental illness is characterised by fragmentation and imbalance with the more recently developed parts of the mind being more vulnerable while health is a simpler state of balance and wholeness.

We have found general qualities of mental health which are important in combatting depression: connectedness, balance, synchrony and transcendence. Connectedness with other people gives us meaningful roles and loving relationships. Balance of rest and activity keeps our stress hormones in check and at a chemical level a stable mood reflects neuro-transmitters in equilibrium. Synchrony between our internal rhythms, especially our circadian cycle, and the outer world is another foundation of positive mood. Transcending can start with just stepping back to review your thinking processes in Cognitive Therapy or undertaking the trickier journey inwards with Psychoanalysis. Simpler but deeper experience is available through Transcendental Meditation.

The path out of depression must start from where you are. It is easier to start when you are not depressed, so as to prevent depression occurring, but that is the wisdom of hindsight. If you are already depressed that is your start line and to get out of the mud you have to start walking through it. You may well need the help of others, family and friends or professionals, at some point.

Your choice of path is guided by what supports you have available and what sort of help or therapy appeals to you. It may be influenced by what you see as the main cause of your depression but this is not as important a reason as you might think. The obvious cause might be losing your job but there may be much stronger elements in place before this sad event such as a constitutional vulnerability, poor routine, negative thinking patterns or previous losses you never came to terms with. Your reason for being depressed may be over-whelming and impossible to deal with directly. A refugee has terrible losses and traumas which cannot be easily or directly repaired and the immediate path to take may involve massage, meditation or medication to help them cope with their depression at least enough to start establishing a new life.

As with heart disease it is useful to address several factors. Most therapies and strategies are not incompatible with each other. It is necessary to keep a clear rationale for what you are doing to improve your mood and remember there is more than one element with which to deal. If you are taking medication and think that this is the only reason you feel better, this will undermine any psychological efforts you are making. If you are too focussed on emotions and relationships you will have less interest in a good sleep pattern. Many therapists are fine with this approach but a few are not. Some treatments do demand more belief and commitment, Psychoanalysis being the prime example as using another method to feel better can be seen by an analyst as avoiding the real psycho-dynamic problems. Most important parts of life are complex and we do have the ability to hold more than one strategy in our mind.

It is also appropriate to monitor your own progress and review your route. If you have already tried three anti-depressants without result and the doctor is suggesting taking additional medicines this may be reasonable from the pharmacological perspective but you should be assessing whether other areas need attention. Are you still hanging out with an alcoholic abusive partner? Even if you do not have such a clear external stressor you may want to add more cognitive and behavioral approaches to your drugs.

We do not choose where we start from but we can decide where we are going and how far we want to go. At least we want to get back to average mood and if possible to a stable enough state of resilience that future depression is unlikely. We can set higher goals and this should not seem odd. Just as in the Middle Ages in Europe being clean would have been odd we now live in an age where having a stress free enlightened mind seems unusual. It should not be so.

First steps: basic self-care

Never neglect the obvious ways of fighting depression and do not concentrate on one emotional cause or life event and excuse yourself from basic self-care. Use family and friends to stay connected to others even if you are not a bundle of fun to be with. Do not become isolated and remote. Reducing work time or family commitments may be better than cutting out completely. If you are one of the support people remember that your company is helpful even if there is not much immediate joy coming back at you.

Keep a good routine with regular eating times and sleep time because your circadian rhythm is critical to mental health. Routines also assist you in managing your level of activity and rest. This includes the balance in each day as well as having weekends and holidays.

Keep to at least a reasonable diet and take regular exercise. Exercise is such a simple easy and cheap therapy. This is an aspect of our life-style that is much better put in place when we are well as when we are low starting up is challenging. If it is already as routine as brushing your teeth and/or you have a hearty group of mates to encourage you it is so much less effort.

Stopping harmful habits is the other important first step. Look at how you deal with stress and see if this includes unhealthy ways such as alcohol or illegal drugs. These are damaging short-term fixes which perpetuate depression. Why even think of taking anti-depressants or paying expensive Psychologists when you are pushing yourself down with depressant drinking? If you are really caught up in addiction then that needs treating in its own right.

The first steps emphasise balance, synchrony and connectedness. The second steps add transcendence.

Second steps: refining and transcending

The next level includes refining the first steps to a deeper level which is good for maintaining health as well as for guiding you out of depression. They involve increasing your knowledge of your-self in a few simple ways. Your daily routine and diet can be fine-tuned to your individual constitution and to the season of the year. This requires some additional information from MAV but is not difficult. Small adjustments to your routine may pay big dividends.

If there are clear on-going stresses these should be evaluated and addressed. Advice from others is very useful here if your depressed state has clouded your judgement. Your job may be too demanding or your partner may be unsupportive but check that it is not just your negative view of the world telling you this. However if your partner seems abusive to everyone else do not continue to tolerate this and blame yourself.

Review your goals and values and see if you can align more activities with what is important to you. This is especially beneficial if you have major constraints on your time from a job which is not well in tune with your values but which you cannot easily change. In the range of your activity make sure you have some outlets for creativity. This need not be writing the great novel and could be baking or gardening. You should also allow your goals to evolve over time which requires a more searching review.

The counter-balance to activity is rest. Enough sleep is good and a vital first step. Next to add are the deep periods of rest in the day by learning TM. There are other ways of resting but none so profound or as well researched. TM gives a deeper rest and one that enlivens the mind.

Third: the step to professional therapy

This is a major transition when you recognise that professional help is needed. Your ability to care for yourself has been overcome. Hopefully with the above steps depression will be less likely but if it has come down on you hard and your own efforts and social supports are not enough to lift the depression you need specialist help. Many people put off getting this help for too long due to stigma or obstinacy. There is nothing wrong with being self-reliant, nothing at all, but we need to make use of available help when suffering is too great or goes on too long. For some of us the most difficult step is actually recognising we are depressed and need help.

The best professional to see first for most people is their family doctor. This visit serves both to cover any physical reasons for being depressed and as a guide to any specialist mental health care. Family doctors see many people with depression but they vary greatly in their knowledge of different options. Definitely they will be familiar with drugs and they should also be familiar with psychological options as well as the basic lifestyle advice. Their ability to give such advice has improved greatly in recent years due to campaigns to treat depression better and earlier.

There are some specific symptoms or types of depression which indicate you will need to see a mental health specialist not just a family doctor. These include Bipolar Disorder because it has a specific course, is a long term illness, and requires different management to other depressions. Any psychotic symptoms such as hallucinations or delusional ideas are indications for more specialised help. Suicidal ideas are another clear warning sign.

If you do not have the above symptoms you should review if you have used enough of the initial strategies to keep your life-style in balance, stay connected to others, and get enough deep rest. Then the main choices are between anti-depressants and psychological therapies. The milder your depression the less good is the risk/benefit ratio for drugs. Conversely the worse your depression the better is the chances. Other reasons for taking the drugs would be previous response or strong family history. If you have a known history of trauma there is more indication for psychological therapy.

For depression at the moderate level or if you prefer not to try the medication there are many psychotherapies on the market. Psychological therapy used to be limited to face to face sessions. Now we have evolved into cyberspace there are more options. Firstly we have access to much more information and advice about self-care on-line. We can proceed to on-line therapy by using CBT programs which can be done anonymously with no human feed-back or for some packages with limited personal advice. At the next level face to face sessions can also be done via our computer screens, but unless you live so remotely that travel to an office is hard most people will choose to attend in person.

CBT is the first-line therapy and may progress to Acceptance and Commitment Therapy if needed. There may be specific skills identified such as problem solving or assertiveness or stress tolerance which need training. If your personality is Borderline then a more comprehensive program like DBT is worth-while. The more complex psycho-dynamic therapies such as Psychoanalysis are problematic. There are not clear indications for them and the outcomes are less evidenced and to succeed you do need to give the dynamic therapies full commitment and this will mean going through some emotional pain in the process.

If anti-depressants are the choice you should still put some attention on other strategies. The drugs will struggle to kick in if you are still drinking eight beers an evening and watching violent movies till 2 a.m. every night. You can consider St John's Wort rather than modern anti-depressants but most practitioners will not be knowledgeable about both. Similarly you can use MAV herbal medicines but MAV specialists do not use modern drugs. With our present knowledge it may be best to use the herbal medicines for less severe depressions where the evidence for the modern drugs is less good. Whichever you use it is good to discuss an exit strategy with your doctor. Six months is the standard advice for a first episode of depression but this is based on an average length episode and your needs may be different. Make sure you set your sights high enough, not just getting to a level at which you can survive.

If you do not get better despite having treatment you can review with your therapist if more is needed or a different type of therapy or more than one therapy. CBT and anti-depressants for example can work well together if the medication gives you more energy and concentration to make use of the psychological help.

The third step involves another person – a doctor or therapist. What sort of relationship you have with them is critical and must be one that supports your involvement and empowerment. The choice of therapy and therapist is illuminated by your tendencies to be the Knower, process of Knowing or Known. Chronic depression is often associated with being stuck in the Known role waiting for others to advise or rescue you. Your path forward will need you to move into the Knowing role to be more active in understanding yourself and also into the Knower role taking responsibility for owning knowledge of your-self and your health. On the other hand if you spend too much time analysing and thinking an action oriented approach will be better.

Fourth steps: managing a long-term tendency to depression

If you have repeated depressions or never seem to fully recover a happy state then other strategies are needed or you need to add more approaches together. Suppose medication gets you out of depression but you relapse each time you stop the drugs. You might just continue on the drugs indefinitely as many people do. This would only be worthwhile if you had a very good level of recovery with very few or no side effects and you would also have to happy with taking the medication of course. You should review all the points in the first two steps. Are there stresses in your life that need resolving rather than tolerating? Are you stuck and need new challenges and goals to pursue?

Self-help groups have a role in supporting people with long term depression. They can give emotional and social support, reduce alienation, reduce the strain on your family and friends, and share ways of coping. It is very wearying to be depressed for long periods when therapy does not seem to work. As well as using any long-term supports available it is also important to keep looking for a path back to health.

Look at your constitution over the course of your life. Are you a Vata type with tendency to anxiety and easily thrown out of rhythm who finds stress hard to endure? Or are you more Pitta driving yourself despite stress and fatigue? Perhaps you are Kapha, more steady and solid needing more activation and exercise? Particularly when therapy has been unsuccessful in keeping you well you can usefully review your constitution and how to balance it, with professional input if needed.

Depressions on top of a persistent variability of mood require careful and correct management. If you have significant higher than normal moods and are diagnosed with Bipolar Disorder, then the usual mix of therapies are mood stabilising medication, close attention to daily routine and sleep, plus a support group of others with Bipolar illness. Remember the caution that anti-depressants can greatly worsen the condition as do most illegal drugs. If however your mood swings are much shorter and you have Borderline Personality Disorder your best bet is psychological therapy such as DBT. Medication is not going to cure you and at best will reduce impulsivity or take the edge off the depression.

Mindfulness has become more accepted as useful in anxiety and depression and is a part of DBT and ACT. This practice seeks to reduce secondary distressing thoughts and reduce the impact of your primary depressive symptoms. TM is a deeper form of meditation whose goal is to go completely beyond any specific thought to the unchanging level of pure awareness. This is a level beyond negativity and a reassuring experience of your Self in its simplest and most secure state. CBT and ACT have their effect from repeatedly stepping back from and reflecting on your surface thoughts. TM cultivates the ability of the mind transcend to more abstract levels so you are permanently less bound up by surface negativity or neurotic inner conversation.

Fifth level: changing society's mood

We know that our mood is affected by those around us. Even distant people in our social network have their influence. The average mood of our culture is low and anxiety, addiction and relationship problems are very common. Each person with depression can seek to improve them-selves and have therapy which is fine but how shall we lift up the average mood, the national mood or even global mood?

Economic progress is good for mood at very low levels of wealth but once you are out of poverty getting richer is disappointingly unhelpful. Connectedness is a potential solution as many of us have lost the nurturing of extended family, tribe or village life. We are connecting as fast as we can on social media and the internet but have not yet found out how best to use these. Balance of rest and activity is well out with part of society working too long hours and another part unemployed. The solutions here may be political but on the level of businesses or institutions we can look at work-life balance and values other than the pursuit of money. Synchrony in life has also slipped ironically because of economic and technological progress. We no longer need the sun to light up our activity but the basics of a natural life-style can be relearned. Transcendence has been lost as a regular experience but again we can easily learn or be reminded of this basic field of life.

While therapy usually appears in adult life we must encourage the teaching of skills and health education in child-hood. One of the reasons therapies for depression may not work so well is that the problems date back so long. Habits and ways of thinking need to be relearned and some basic skills have never been learned. These include essential abilities like problem solving and distress tolerance.

The most natural ability that has not been exercised is our ability to transcend the relative levels of thought and feeling and to just be our Self. The deeper levels of our mind are more powerful and more positive and blissful. Established in the transcendent our mental abilities increase to allow much stronger meta-cognition or reflective functioning and the integration of different modes of experience. With proper development of the mind we can have a strong foundation of mental health and progress not just away from depression but towards enlightenment. The important lessons of BT are that learning is easy and we can progress to more elevated goals. Information and feedback are necessary. This underlines the importance of education in describing the goals of life and the path to achieve them.

It is excellent that the goal of recovery from severe mental illness is now a life worth living and that this is defined as being more than just an average life. For the general population there is much more interest in physical fitness and increasingly in mental potential as well. Escaping from depression or anxiety or addiction are worthy endeavours but we should also recognize the higher goal of enlightenment to enjoy the infinite span of existence being lively in every moment. The unique gift of human life is that our nervous system allows the individual to experience and reflect the life of the universe. Aiming at lower goals than this is one reason why our search for Agent Blue has been inconclusive.

There has also been more recognition by governments that all areas of life affect mental health and that depression in particular has a great effect on society. Unemployment stresses one's mood and depression taking people out of work is a drain on the economy. Housing, education, arts, culture, religion all relate strongly to mental health. It is becoming fashionable to look for a cross sector or "whole of government" approach to mental health in the recognition that the health service alone is not sufficient to deal with problems like depression. There is no health without mental health and no area of society can be truly successful without strength in our mental life. The general importance of mental health is now recognised but its primacy as the basis of societal success needs to be underlined. It is much harder for an individual to avoid depression when the society in which he or she lives is itself depressed.

Expecting Bliss

The nature of life is to reverberate between the wholeness of the underlying Unified Field of consciousness and the diversity on the surface of life. As individuals we experience both sides. We value our independence but we also desire integration, connectedness and love. In modern times there has been over emphasis on the outer material aspects of success and not enough attention on our deeper values and inner experience. To find balance and connectedness in life we need to have the more expanded and intelligent basis of the mind open to us. Self knowledge supports better thinking and behavior.

Growing up into a stable and happy life requires us to learn skills and also to become mature. Schools do not need to be full of disciplinary and behavioral problems. Children should be living learning in an atmosphere of coherence and harmony. From a young age we need to ensure they have regular periods of quiet to balance their natural exuberance and activity.

In adolescence dependency on others is both desired and resisted. When the mind and self are not based on a secure foundation this dilemma becomes painful and unresolved. This is reflected in the immaturity of relationships in society and the frequency of Borderline personality traits. Adolescence is a time when our individuality has to negotiate our desire for intimate relationships and finding our place in society, and it is not being well managed at present. This important time of transition is not producing adults who can easily maintain both their own independence and strong connectedness with their friends, families, and society. Depression anxiety and addiction are the unfortunate consequences.

The same problem is seen at the national level with too much selfish political and economic strategy. We need to move up from promoting the needs of individual countries to working globally and producing the best environment for all countries. Global action in health is possible. The successful campaign against smallpox was an excellent example which showed the importance of working at the level of society not just the individual. In mental health we also have to think globally. We are all connected by cyberspace and by economics and our global culture is growing fast. The internet and social media can be great avenues for progress in a campaign to lift global mood, but we shall need to expand and deepen our internal world to support all the expansion in our external relationships and activities. To do this we must fulfil our mental potential and remember our natural ability to experience the most settled state of consciousness which is the underlying field of the mind.

Our challenge is for global consciousness and maturity to grow and support not just life free from depression but a life truly worth living, a life of bliss. We do have the technologies and strategies to achieve this. Now is the time for lifting the global mood and achieving a more normal more blissful level of consciousness. As individuals we naturally want to be free from depression and we have seen there are many paths available. We can address the different factors underlying depression and move ahead to strengthening our minds and becoming more mature resilient enlightened people. Then we can enjoy life to the maximum and contribute most to the world around us.

∞∞∞

Appendix 1   Constitution Questionnaire:

Circle YES for all items that describe you as you have usually been throughout most of your adult life.

Walk very quickly	YES		
Thick, luxuriant, oily hair			YES
Dry rough skin	YES		
Reddish or freckled skin		YES	
Moist, oily skin			YES
Small teeth	YES		
Yellowish teeth		YES	
Large body frame			YES
Penetrating eyes		YES	
Quick, restless mind	YES		
Sharp intellect, aggressive		YES	
Calm, steady mind			YES
Thin, tend not to put on weight	YES		
Medium weight		YES	
Heavy, tend to put on weight easily			YES
Small body frame	YES		
Strong, large white teeth			YES
Dislike hot weather		YES	
Short-term memory better than long-term	YES		
Good overall memory		YES	
Sound sleep of average length		YES	
Sound heavy and long sleep			YES
Good appetite, cannot skip meals easily		YES	
Tend to be constipated, hard stools	YES		
Low strength and stamina	YES		
High stamina for exercise			YES
Physically very strong			YES
Easily excitable	YES		
Tend to get angry, lose temper under stress		YES	
Slow to get irritated			YES
Add the total for each column			
Doshas:	**Vata**	**Pitta**	**Kapha**

Add the total for each Dosha: VATA   PITTA   KAPHA   to have an estimate of your constitutional profile.

Appendices

Appendix 2   Influences on the Three Doshas

Factors tending to increase or aggravate VATA
Dry, cold, windy weather
Early morning and late afternoon
Old age
Irregular routines
Insufficient sleep
Suppression of natural urges
Weight loss
Falling
Excessive speaking
Excessive travel
Excessive exercise
Too little or irregular meals
Light, dry and cold food
Pungent, bitter, astringent tastes

Factors tending to increase or aggravate PITTA
Hot weather
Excessive sun
Midday and midnight
Middle age
Late bed-time
Anger
Alcohol
Tobacco
Hot food and drink
Pungent sour and salty tastes

Factors tending to increase or aggravate KAPHA
Cold, wet weather
Morning and evening
Childhood
Excessive sleep
Too little exercise
Too little work or mental activity
Excessive food, cold food and drink
Sweet, sour and salty tastes

Further Reading

By the Author
From Anxiety to Peace, Choosing a Therapy for Anxiety and Panic. Nick Argyle. Grayle Books 2012.

Transcendental Meditation
Transcendence: Healing and Transformation through TM. Norman E Rosenthal. Penguin 2011.
www.mum.edu/tm_research/research.html

Enlightenment
Science of Being and Art of Living: Transcendental Meditation. Maharishi Mahesh Yogi. Penguin 2001.
Maharishi's Absolute Theory of Government. 1995. Maharishi Prakashan.
Human Physiology: Expression of the Veda and the Vedic Literature. Tony Nader. 1995 Maharishi Vedic University.
Growing up Enlightened. Randi Nidich. MIU Press 1990.
www.mum.edu/m_effect/index.html

General
Consciousness. Susan Blackmore. Oxford University Press 2005.
www.whatthebleep.com/ (Modern Physics)
www.nimh.nih.gov/health/topics/depression (National Institute of Mental Health Overview.)
http://www.blackdoginstitute.org.au (Australian campaign site.)

Behavior Therapy
http://psychology.tools/behavioral-activation.html (self help sheets.)
Control Your Depression, Revised Ed. Peter Lewinsohn. (includes other cognitive methods) Touchstone 1992.

Cognitive Therapy
Learned Optimism. Martin Seligman. Knopf 1991.

Cognitive Therapy and the Emotional Disorders. Aaron T Beck. Meridian 1979.
http://cognitivetherapyonline.com
http://www.ccbt.co.uk/ (on-line mainly CBT, includes OCD.)

Psychoanalysis and Dynamic Therapy
The Interpretation of Dreams. Sigmund Freud. Macmillan 1913.
Memories Dreams and Reflections. Carl Jung. Collins 1961.
On Becoming a Person. Carl Rogers. Constable 1961.

Biological Therapy
www.nice.org.uk/guidance/cg90/chapter/1-guidance (UK clinical guidelines including anti-depressants.)

Manic Depression
The Depression Workbook: A Guide for Living with Depression and Manic Depression. Mary Ellen Copeland. 2002.

Group Therapy
The Group Therapy Experience: From Theory to Practice. Dr. Louis R. Ormont. Book Surge Publishing 2009.

Natural Medicine
Dealing with Depression Naturally: Complementary and Alternative Therapies for Restoring Emotional Health. Syd Baumel. Keats Publishing 2000.

Maharishi Ayurveda
A Woman's Best Medicine. Nancy Lonsdorf. Putnam 1993.
Perfect Health . Deepak Chopra. Harmony 2001.
www.alltm.org/ayurveda.html

Enlightened Building and Town Planning
www.sthapatyaveda.com/

www.ingramcontent.com/pod-product-compliance
Lightning Source LLC
Chambersburg PA
CBHW021156160426
43194CB00007B/763